WHAT PEOPLE ARE SAYING ABC

Thank you so much for taking th
to write these Messages for people like
become much calmer and feel more s
everyday spiritual food.

—Roumyana Petrova
Assistant Professor, Dept. of European Studies, Bulgaria

The [Messages] have totally changed my life. They have explained the many changes, feelings and emotions that I have been experiencing over the last 3 years. I can't begin to find the words that will express my heartfelt thanks for what I have learnt and gained.

—Dave Elliott, England

When I think about the Messages, three words come immediately to my mind—love, gratitude and hope. I *feel* an almost indescribable love coming from the Hosts of Heaven when I read their words. I am oh so very grateful to the Hosts of Heaven for putting this information out and to my soul for guiding me to it.

—Ginny Burgess, North Carolina, USA

I have read channeled material from various sources throughout the world, but none have brought home to me the true purpose of my existence on Earth as clearly as the *Operation Terra* Messages. These Messages have changed my life and made sense of all that has gone before.

—Kevin Haupt, N.Dip Elec. Eng., Buckinghamshire, England

Thank you for the wonderful Messages. I appreciate them very much, particularly in these turbulent times.

—J.D. Bloom, Unity School of Christianity, Missouri, USA

In these lightning-speed changes happening in the world today, it was such a blessing and a relief to come across *Operation Terra*. Every word is an affirmation and strengthening for my soul to hear. Thank you, thank you, thank you!

—Susie Ekberg, Reiki Master, North Dakota, USA

The truth in these Messages will awaken, uplift and inspire all who read them to stay steadfast in anchoring the love and light, as we move through a process and time that has not occurred on Planet Earth before. A must read for all lightworkers!

—Joya, Los Angeles, USA

All my life I knew I was from someplace else because I did not fit in anywhere on this planet. My wakeup call came on September 11, 2001 when I found the *Operation Terra* material, and it was a direct Message from the Hosts of Heaven, calling me home.

—Madonna Spitzmiller, Fort Lauderdale, Florida, USA

I believe that 9/11 has had a "jarring" effect on many people, though not perhaps for all the same reasons. For me, it's meant a kind of "crossing over," like standing suddenly on the opposite side of a river. I have even said to friends, "Everything is different now!" All I can say is, thank God for you and your message. It is saving my life.

—Peter Brackett, Atlanta, Georgia, USA

This morning [Sept. 15, 2001] I found myself thinking, well, there's always suicide. I don't HAVE to stay here. But after reading your amazingly calming and clear words, my perspective has shifted completely, and I have reconnected with what I call my "place of joy." Thank you oh so very much. I am at peace again.

—Terrie Osborn, Syracuse, New York, USA

When I started reading the Messages, I would find myself at times so moved—tears overflowing, completely overwhelmed in a flood of such peace and comfort it was like a confirmation for me about my spiritual journey. I feel I am ready to face and accept whatever God has planned for me. Thank you again for sharing your gifts of peace, love and encouragement.

—Judy, British Columbia, Canada

Upon discovering the Messages from the Hosts of Heaven, I experienced a resonance which brought me incredible joy! I was guided, encouraged, and uplifted. *Operation Terra* is a blessing to all!!!

—Krista Jones, Administrative Assistant, Ivy Tech State College
South Bend, Indiana, USA

Operation Terra has removed the fear factor from my life. I am recommending this book to my spirit groups and my loved ones, so they too can be enlightened. Thank you, Lyara, for your wonderful gift.

—Barbara Nye Bivens, owner of Drastic Changes, Bastrop, Texas, USA

To me, the Messages from the Hosts have a ring of quiet authenticity to them, a clear tone, a harmonic and comforting resonance. I thank you for your service. Every Message is a true Work of Art.

—Brennan G Allen, Lecturer
University of Waikato, New Zealand

If you're "different" and long to inhabit a planet of love, beauty, peace, and joy, then these Messages are for you. ... Light codes *are* imbedded in the text and *will* activate resonance that is within you, bringing forth forgotten missions, dreams, visions, and connections that join similar ones held by others, ultimately lifting all of this family and Earth herself to 4D Terra. After decades of searching, these Messages offer truth, guidance and courage I've not found elsewhere. This ET is going home!

—Lily Jay, writer, Colorado, USA

I really have enjoyed [*Operation Terra*]. I had been looking for this information for quite a while. It's like finally being told what the bigger picture is that I've always felt deep down, but never talked about. I'm glad you've put forth these Messages to people like me who are searching for the ultimate vision of what they want and have chosen their life to be. I thank you for everything you have done and I'm glad I found this place...   —Tanner Guse, Canada

I'm not a very emotional person. The usual love stories don't reach me, but when I read the [Messages], it was like reading what I was like and what I have believed in all my life. At last something told me why I have been so different all my life. Chills went up and down my spine and tears came to my eyes over and over again. I felt blessed.
                     —Petri Filipczak, software engineer, Finland

The material from *Operation Terra* has changed the way in which I view life, humanity, spirituality and our planet. It reveals the true meaning of current world events and how these are reflective of the end of the current paradigm and the beginning of a new one. This knowledge has provided me a sense of love and peace with the understanding that no matter what our experience, it is for the highest light and divine order of all.
                     —Burton Gazzara, Feng Shui consultant, Los Angeles, California, USA

Operation Terra has changed my life. Where I was full of doubt and confusion, I am now overflowing with love and gratitude. Thank you so much for revealing these truths in such an easy-to-understand style.   —Toni Broughton, British Columbia, Canada

You and your guides are so clear, it is good indeed. Thanks for the wonderful Messages.
                     —Rev. Linda Ann Stancombe, Demorest, Georgia, USA

We are in the middle of the most incredible event of our physical and spiritual history. The *Operation Terra* Messages offer clarity and comfort to those who want to know more about these unprecedented times.   —Rob Glenesk, artist and teacher, Canada

The Messages channeled through you have helped me in so many ways, and have made me see things in a much broader perspective that even that alone is already a gift. Thank you, and thank God.
                     —Cherry Diao, Philippines

Know that you and your work are appreciated far and near. I have had the honor of seeing ships, the split, the New Earth, the new bodies, the coming life. The integrity and discipline required of us to be included there are significant. Thanking you deeply,
                     —Dianne, Costa Rica

I want to thank you and the "Hosts" with all my heart for your wonderful book!!! Your messages totally confirm what I've been getting since the late '60s. Thank you from the depth of my soul!

—Louise Nason, USA

I want to thank you from the bottom of my heart for the work that you have done. Your information is the best channeled material I have ever come across. Your latest Messages have been very—I mean *very* accurate (it's almost scary) about the latest events in the news. Once again, thank you.

—Patrick Mandelin, Alberta, Canada.

I cannot begin to express how much peace and hope these Messages of love have brought to me. Thank you, thank you, thank you. I cried as I read some of these Messages, for they were written as if out of the very "pages" of my own soul.

—Pamela Howard, Alaska, USA

I found these Messages amazing and uplifting. The material gave me more than just hope: it seemed to fit like pieces of a puzzle I thought had something missing. Never before has something felt right and so simply fitting as this! I want to thank you and your group for the help.

—Thomas Wilcox, Oregon, USA

[These] Messages provide comfort and grace in a time of such uncertainty and seeming "chaos" in the world. We are truly part of a Divine Plan, and this book reminds us of how much we are loved and protected by the Hosts of Heaven. I recommend this book to all lightworkers who are seeking peace, love and joy.

—Janet Houser, author of *Self-Mastery Through the Twelve Rays*

The *Operation Terra* Messages fit me better than anything else I've read in the vast arena of spiritual information. *Operation Terra* has been what I was searching for, over many years. Your work has been a true benefit to many such "lost souls" as myself.

—Brad Becker, Arkansas, USA

I have just finished reading through the end of Vol. 2 and all the articles. I have never resonated with anything as strongly as I resonate with this information. My body was ALIVE, with every inch, from head to toe, tingling with excitement. Thank you.

—Amy Topham, USA

The Hosts of Heaven are preparing us. I felt their grace, and responded with love, peace, delight, and thanks. My whole body shivered, and the resonance with these Messages made me cry. Thank you for these Messages.

——Chang-Soo Jeon, novelist, Seoul, Korea

OPERATION TERRA

MESSAGES FROM THE HOSTS OF HEAVEN

*A new revelation on Earth changes, ETs, the end times, and
the journey to the New Earth, Terra*

VOLUME TWO

as received by
SARA LYARA ESTES

CELESTIAL WAY
USA

OPERATION TERRA
MESSAGES FROM THE HOSTS OF HEAVEN
*A new revelation on Earth changes, ETs, the end times,
and the journey to the New Earth, Terra*
VOLUME TWO

© Copyright 2001–2003 Sara Lyara Estes. All rights reserved.
Published 2002. Second edition 2003. Revised edition 2005.

07 06 05   9 8 7 6 5 4 3

COVER, TYPOGRAPHY AND DESIGN BY SARA LYARA ESTES

Publisher's Cataloging-in-Publication

Estes, Sara Lyara.
    Operation Terra. Volume Two : messages from the Hosts of Heaven: a new revelation on Earth changes, ETs, the end times, and the journey to the new Earth, Terra / Sara Lyara Estes.
    p. ; cm.
    Includes bibliographical references.
    LCCN 2001117583
    ISBN 0-9711297-2-X
    1. End of the world. 2. Prophecies.
3. Spirituality. I. Title. II. Title: Messages from the Hosts of Heaven
BT876.E88 2001   236'.9

Published by CELESTIAL WAY
USA
Printed on acid-free paper in the USA

Dedicated to
the Operation Terra family,
wherever they may be.

ABOUT VOLUMES TWO & THREE

There is no question in anyone's mind that the world changed dramatically on September 11, 2001. On September 8, 2001, the Hosts made an uncharacteristic statement in the Message entitled, "The Time of Ingathering," which is included in Volume Two. They said, simply enough, "...you—as a planetary population—are about to enter a time of deepening strife and travail." The attacks on the World Trade Center and the Pentagon occurred 2½ days later. To the best of my knowledge, that Message was the only source of publicly available information that accurately forecast those events.

Immediately after the shock of that fateful day, the Hosts were there for us again, delivering a relatively rapid series of Messages to offer comfort and a positive frame of reference within which to view the events that have unfolded since then. From the letters I received during that timeframe, those Messages truly saved lives and helped many people cope in a world gone mad. It was truly a wakeup call for humanity and many have since found a haven in the Operation Terra material and philosophy.

Unfolding world events now unmistakenly bear out the truth of the prophecies made in this book. Volume Two picks up where Volume One leaves off and takes us around the next turn on the spiral, lifting us and our understanding to a higher, yet deeper level, and lovingly charts our course through the stormy seas of change.

In response to an acceleration in the efforts of the "loyal opposition," Volume Three was abruptly discontinued on May 6, 2005 due to the Hosts' concern to remove the first and second waves from the planet before the end of December, 2005.

The Messages for Volume Three are only available through the Operation Terra Web site at www.operationterra.com. Volumes One and Two can be ordered on the Web through Amazon.com throughout the world, or may be ordered through your local bookstore, if you prefer.

I wish you well on your journey, wherever it may lead and whatever form it may take. Many blessings to you and yours.

—Sara Lyara Estes
July 18, 2005

PREFACE TO THE SECOND EDITION

I began shipping the first edition of Volume Two in the first week of December, 2002. Barely three weeks later, a reader in Canada pointed out to me that an entire Message, "Calm, Grounded, and Centered," was missing from the book. I was stunned. I considered several options to correct the error, none of which were practical or met the needs for all situations. A few days later, another reader wrote and informed me that the "Clarification" for "Calm, Grounded, and Centered" was pasted on to the end of "The God Game," where it made no sense whatsoever. The last week of December was not a happy time for me, and I further agonized as the "Booster Rocket" event that the Hosts had said would occur "later this year" had not come to pass by January 1, 2003. My greatest fear in being a channel had been that I would be unintentionally used by negative-polarity sources to give false information to those who placed their faith in what I was being asked to share. I do not want to be a "false prophet" because I do not want to be a source of pain, loss or discouragement for anyone else; however, I have no choice but to do the best I can to discern the source of my information and then turn the rest over to God.

In the 18+ years of training I went through before the Hosts asked me to deliver the first Messages in mid-1999, I did not share my channelings with anyone else except my closest friends. If I had been given false information during that time—if I had not been able to accurately discern the source of what came through me—I felt relatively safe about that because I would not harm anyone but myself. However, once I was asked to deliver the Messages in a way that other people would read them and be affected by them, I felt a growing responsibility toward my readers, and my concern grew about being a source of potentially false information that could cause harm to others. My turmoil during the last week of December 2002 put me through a crisis of faith. Despite the fact that the Hosts were the only source of inspired information that accurately predicted 9/11 before it occurred, the same fear comes up each and every time I am called upon to channel: "It has worked before, but will it work now?" It's a little like perpetual "stage fright" each time and nothing I do seems to make it go away, no matter how much I release attachments to any particular outcome. The Messages emphasize the importance of facing down our fears. I am not exempt from this requirement, and like everyone else, I have to do this over and over again. I know that the particular Message that was missing in the first edition of Volume Two had been in the file that I used to construct the typeset book. Somewhere along the line it disappeared, and I simply did not notice it because I was so focused on the details of correct punctuation, spelling, chapter headings, etc. that I did not notice the larger error. That in itself is a good lesson—to be so focused on the details causes us to lose sight of the "big picture," and that's exactly what happened to me.

The pressure reached its maximum on January 4, 2003, when I began to get letters from people who wanted to know why the Booster Rocket event had not happened as the Hosts had said it would. Before I went to bed that night, I was determined to get an answer from the Hosts, who had previously told me only that "all would be well." They gave me a firm answer that made sense to me, and I wrote the article "On Being Pioneers," which is now part of this book. I put it up on the site and sent out a letter to my e-mail list. The response was an astonishing outpouring of love and support, accompanied by a few letters of chastisement about having taking myself too seriously, and some people leaving my list in dissatisfaction. The vast majority of people said that they had already learned to not take dates as cast in stone, and that the vibration of truth that they found in the Messages far outweighed any details that might not be totally correct. I saw that they were not quite as vulnerable to my mistakes as I had thought they were. In Biblical times, a prophet would be stoned to death for making even one prediction that failed to come to pass. It does seem that we have progressed a bit since that time—that we have become a little more responsible for our OWN truth and have learned to take what is valuable and to leave the rest, no matter where we have found it. It is in that spirit that I humbly offer you this new edition and hope it is of value to you.

—Sara Lyara Estes
January 9, 2003

CONTENTS

SUPPLEMENTARY MATERIAL

Have you noticed a certain sense of unreality these days? Have you seen with different perception? Do things look a little unreal to you? Good. Then everything is just as it should be. You are beginning to see things as the projections that they are.

GO WITH THE FLOW:
Becoming One with the Mind of God
March 26, 2001

All right, now. We have asked to speak with you today because of certain concepts that are lacking in your awareness that are important for you to understand before proceeding much further in your transformation. We would say that you can transform without this understanding, but we feel it is easier for you to cooperate with the changes if you understand them ahead of time, so when things begin to occur, you can say, "Oh, so *that's* what that is!" and that will make it easier for you to release into the experience, because the known is never as frightening as the unknown.

So, now, where are you in the process? Where are you with all these pronouncements of dates and shifts and gates and the like? If you choose to focus on these phenomena, you will miss what's important. What's important is what's going on beneath the surface, tucked away from prying eyes and safely hidden within the deepest levels of your self. It is there, in your secret temple, that you can meet with your Creator, undisturbed and uninterrupted and face-to-face. We would like you to cultivate that as your primary place of meeting.

To be sure, it is helpful when one is going through so many changes, especially ones that one doesn't understand—it is natural and understandable that you would reach out to others, to see if you are the only one that is experiencing these things, and when you find out that you are in good company, then you can relax and say, "Ah, it isn't just me." However, as we have said before, there really is only ONE Being that is doing all this experiencing, and it is part of your shift into the consciousness of Terra for you to begin to experience this—not as a concept, but as a felt and real thing within yourself.

Have you noticed a certain sense of unreality these days? Have you seen with different perception? Do things look a little unreal to you? Good. Then everything is just as it should be. You are beginning to see things as the projections that they are. Let us back up to the hologram that we spoke of some time ago. A hologram is created by two beams of coherent light. One is called the reference beam and is constant. The other is called the "working beam" and it plays out different patterns on the reference beam. The INTERACTION between these two beams creates patterns of light and dark that are a result of the beams either adding to each other (in phase) or subtracting from one another (out of phase), to one degree or another. If the two beams are completely in phase, there is an amplification of the light and if the two beams are completely out of phase, there is a cancellation of the light. Relationships in between those two extremes result in light of different strengths, or what you might refer to as shadows.

The Source of all Creation is the reference beam. It is constant and is the only Absolute that there is. Everything else is RELATIVE to that reference beam and interacts with it to create the patterns of form that you perceive with your senses. The Creator projects the "other," which is still part of the Creator, but provides the mechanism to interact with the reference beam so that all the variations can be experienced. To the degree that one is aligned with the Creator (the reference beam), to that degree the interference patterns of light and shadow are diminished until the working beam and the reference beam are totally in phase and all there is is light. The extreme opposite would be an energy or force or entity that is totally out of phase with the Creator and the result would be the cancellation of the light, or the total absence of light—what you refer to as darkness. There is very little to be found in your present reality that is pure light or pure absence of light. Most things are somewhere in between.

You are in the process of becoming totally aligned with the Creator. That is why Terra will be as it will be—everything on it will be in total oneness with the Creator. Every particle of matter will be in oneness with the Creator. There will be no experience of separation and there will only be the Will of the Creator manifesting in perfection. This is why your cellular memory is gradually being purged—so that you can release all your attachments to your experience of being separate in any way from anyone or anything else. All the "shadows" within you are being flooded with light from the highest source, and all that is not in alignment with the Creator is being flushed out as the amount of light increases within your bodies. These emissions from your sun are one mechanism for adding to the quantity of light contained in the matter that makes up Earth and its inhabitants. The sun acts as a lens to step down the higher light and acts to store the energy for a time until it reaches a threshold and then a burst occurs, sending a new impulse of light toward the planet and driving it deep within the atomic structure of all forms that exist upon and around the planet. This absorption of energy within the atoms will eventually lead to what is called a quantum leap—the electrons will jump orbits and release photons and the matter will be transformed into a higher frequency band of reality.

On the way to this glorious explosion, all that is not in alignment with the Creator will be purged. The final stages of the Earth's transformation will not allow present life forms to exist upon her, so they will either be physically lifted or will be removed in other ways, such as through the portal of physical death (dropping the physical body) or through the mechanism of parallel worlds. Those who are not going to Terra and who are not destined to die at this time will experience other things on other parallel "Earths," and it is not necessary for you to know about all these other paths. It is only necessary that you accept your own transformation and the change in consciousness that will accompany it.

Now we want to give you a glimpse of what that will be like, so that you can begin to relate everything else to the change you are making—from a being that experiences separation to a being that is totally at one with all of Creation. Imagine a thick liquid, one that has no form of its own, but which has enough substance to pile up in thick heaps if contained. Now think of an infinitely large container, spread out in all directions as far as you can perceive. You cannot see the far edges of the container, only that it is vast. Now imagine this thick liquid as being able to take on any form that can be imagined, solely through the act of imagining it. That will begin to give you a sense of how the Creator creates.

The Creator exists as a thick matrix that interpenetrates and underlies all form. Your physical senses and instruments cannot measure it or perceive it directly, but when you are in your new consciousness, you will experience yourself as WEARING it, like you would a large bowl of thick fluid, out of which YOU emerge as a similarly fluid being. Your metaphysical teachings say that as one goes higher up on the frequency scale, material substance becomes finer and finer, and that is true. However, there is also a SPIRITUAL mass involved that is in an inverse relationship to the material mass. As material mass DECREASES, spiritual mass INCREASES. At the level of the Creator, there is nothing EXCEPT spirit or intelligent energy and there is "no thing" else. You are perhaps familiar with the equation for converting mass to energy ($E=MC^2$). It shows that there is an enormous amount of energy contained in a given unit of material mass. However, when we are comparing SPIRITUAL mass to material mass, there is a virtual OCEAN of energy available for every minute particle of material form, because it is all connected and any single point of reference is but a particle floating in the ocean of consciousness that contains and surrounds ALL form. There are no discontinuities in that ocean, so the entire ocean is available to any given point within it, at all times.

On Terra, you will experience yourself AND the entire ocean, all at the same time. You have begun to experience this in some ways—perhaps in your meditations or reveries, perhaps if you ingested certain chemicals that affected the filters in your brains so that you could perceive beyond the limitations of your physical senses. You will be in total oneness with the reference beam, and you will only exist as that beam plays on your perceptual screen.

It is that way now, to a certain extent, but there it will be total, conscious (instead of unconscious or dimly perceived), and a permanent state of being.

Everything will be very fluid and gel-like. There will be flow, but no "hard edges." Boundaries that you rely upon now will not exist. You have no idea how much you rely on edges and lines and other demarcations to be able to tell what is where and how to relate to it. You define yourself as a container bounded by your skin. You look in the mirror and define yourself by what you see, and if you don't, the image makes no sense to you. You regard things like shapeshifting with awe, discomfort, or fear because you rely so much on the illusion of a fixed reality. Your physical senses fool you into thinking that if you can't touch it and feel it with your hand, it isn't real. Your culture controls you and keeps you in a box by ridiculing the subtle senses as being "only your imagination" or even worse, labeling it as a pathological condition—a "disease" that has to be cured by cutting it out (lobotomy), shutting it down (drugs and sedatives), or isolating it (institutionalization)—all means of suppression and denial of what is your natural way of being.

We are here to say to you that the world you will inherit is the natural estate of a fully God-conscious entity, whether it is a rock, a tree, a bird, a flower, or a human being. You have been taught that other forms are "lower," that they have no souls or awareness. We are saying just the opposite. ALL form is "informed" by Spirit, by the matrix of the Creator's Mind. All form is conscious and exists within the ocean of consciousness that is the Mind of the Creator. Everything is conscious and everything is exploring life, only in different ways and at different rates. The lifespan of a rock is very long and its processes are comparatively slow. The lifespan of a tree is shorter and the lifespan of a human is shorter still. But each of these things is conscious and each of them has a plan for its existence. The entire Creation interacts with itself, dancing with all the parts like mirrors reflecting the light back and forth between them. It is this dance and the reflections that cause the different patterns of light and shadow, that manifest the expression of all the potentials, so that all paths, all possibilities within a given set of parameters is explored.

So now you are being prepared to go to the next level, where your veils will be dropped and you will experience yourself in your true nature—as conscious projections of the Mind of God, as conscious extensions of the Will of God, and as joyous participants in the dance of Creation, totally aligned with God, and totally of the light. No more "shadow play" on the illusory screen of material reality! You are going "home" to your true estate and you will feast on the riches of the kingdom: peace, joy and love are your true inheritance and you shall have those things and more, in unlimited abundance. As you proceed through the next steps of your transformation, your awareness will begin to shift even more than it has now. Trust that process and do not take it as something that has to be "fixed." You are moving out of a "fixed" reality into a fluid reality, where all potentials exist simultaneously, so you will have to let go and surrender more and more as things proceed. Think of yourself as a cork floating in an ocean of consciousness, bathed in love and light and grace-filled. Let yourself go into this release and feel the peace and the bliss that accompanies the letting go. Let yourself be lifted and carried and let yourself melt and be like a clear stream of the purest water. Ask not where your journey takes you, but just become the flow and it will all unfold perfectly, for you and for all. Go with the flow!

We leave you now in peace and honor and blessing. Amen, Adonoy Sabayoth. We are the Hosts of Heaven. We shall speak with you again.

THE BEST MEDICINE
April 6, 2001

Well, now. Our representative on Earth has asked us to give you some information regarding the experiences you are each having as the cleansing proceeds and you are being lifted free from the underpinnings of that life that you have been experiencing while you have been under the illusion of being physical beings, walking around on the surface of the planet, just like everyone else you see around you. And yet, you have not ever FELT like everyone else around you, have you? You have always felt a little different, although here and there you met up with someone who was like you, only to have them disappear from your life as mysteriously as they had arrived.

We are here to tell you today that you are NOT just a physical body, and that you are different in some very significant ways from everyone else around you—or at least the majority of those around you, because now some of you are partnered with others with whom you share this common heritage. "What heritage?" you may ask. Ahhh. Now it comes down to our revealing one of our "secrets." You see, you are one of us. You are one of those who came together in the beginning to form an alliance, out of which this world that you now walk upon was created. You have felt this special relationship to this planet, because she is in reality to you as a child to a parent. She is your creation and you love her with all of your being, and it pains you to see what is being done to her,

21

especially now, as the final days of greed and self-interest seek to take every last scrap that can be taken before it is all gone.

Dear ones, you are one of us. You speak of the Earth as your mother, but in reality YOU are the parent, and you have a responsibility to your creation—to see her through her birthing onto the next platform of her existence, in the long spiral upward toward Source. When she is safely established in her new reality and the new stewards for her journey have "arrived" and taken over the reins, we will all be complete with our arrangement and go on to other creative endeavors in the vast fields of possibilities that are available. We will sever our alliance as co-creators of THIS reality and go on to form other alliances, for other purposes and to fulfill other desires in the search for experiences on behalf of the Creator of us all.

Now, then, how does all of this relate to what you are experiencing now? How does it relate to the feelings you are having and the body changes you are experiencing? Well, we ask you to let us tell you a little story of sorts, a kind of metaphor to use to understand what exactly is going on. You are not the body you occupy. You are a vast field of intelligent energy that has projected yourself down through all of what you refer to as "dimensions" (that is not an accurate term, but it is what you understand, so we will use that for now) and poured all of that into a very tiny container, the size of a thimble, trying to contain an ocean. There even is a children's story called Thumbelina, which tries to address the experience of being so very tiny in a very vast and enormous world. Let us tell you then the story of Thimble, the very tiny container that you are, and the ocean of consciousness that you are trying to navigate from the perspective of a thimble, floating at sea in a vast ocean of experience.

Thimble is the name we will give you as the central character in our story. We will make Thimble feminine, but that is only to balance all the stories that had masculine central characters. Remember that this is a parable and the meaning is only understood intuitively and not to be taken literally. Let us begin our story:

One day, Thimble woke up. She had been sleeping a long time, rocked to sleep by the eternal movement of the waves on which she floated, a tiny object floating on the vast ocean, far from any shore or sign of land. In her sleep, she was not aware of anything but her dreams, but now that she had awakened, she was aware of being so small and so far away from anything but the vast stretches of ocean that she saw all around her. She had no means of navigation and felt lost and helpless as she perceived her situation. "Where are all the other thimbles?" she wondered. "Surely I can't be the only one like myself. How can I find the others? Am I destined to only float about on this ocean? Is there nothing more?"

Thimble was distressed. She had been so content in her dreams, in which she lived a full life, surrounded by many like herself, able to be just who she was and to have everyone and everything around her be just who they were. It had all been so harmonious, but now what was she to do? Now she appeared to be all alone. Where were the others she had dreamed about and how could she find her way back into that world of her dreams? How had she come to be here, alone on this vast ocean, with no one to speak to, no one with whom she could share the world of her dreams?

Thimble was now very unhappy, but she was also determined to find her way out of the situation in which she found herself. She was determined to find the others and to find her way back to the world of her dreams. But how could she do that? How could she navigate this vast sea and where would she go? There was certainly no sign of land anywhere and no means of getting there, even if she could have seen some. So Thimble prayed. She was self-aware and she knew there was a Thimble-maker somewhere, or she wouldn't have existed at all. "Great Thimble-maker, please help me. I am alone and lost on this vast sea and I want to be back in the world of my dreams. Please send me the means to get there."

So Thimble sent up her prayer and the Great Thimble-maker heard her and sent a beautiful white bird to pick her up and carry her to the world of her dreams, which lay beyond her ability to see it from where she was. Then Thimble was rejoined with those of her kind and she lived happily ever after, awake and aware and surrounded by all the beauty that she loved.

So, my dear ones, I have heard your call and I will send my beautiful white birds to pick you up and take you to the world of your dreams, where you can live happily ever after, awake and aware and surrounded by the beauty that you love.

I now speak to you in the singular because I am the only one here. I am the Thimble-maker AND the Thimble. I am the Hosts of Heaven and so are you. This idea of there being anything else is something I made up, and it has served me well, for otherwise what else was there for me to do? I have been pretending that I am different parts, interacting with other parts, but now it is time for Thimble to wake up to her connection with the Thimble-maker, and so it is necessary to shed all of those parts of herself that are not in keeping with that truth: she and the Thimble-maker are one. Does that ring a bell? Someone else said something like that around 2,000 years ago, and it was not understood then by very many. Only those who had the same experience of oneness that he had could understand what he really meant when he said that, and there were not many of those around at that time. Indeed, there are not many of those around right now, but that is about to change. By the way, if you do happen to hear of someone claiming to have already ascended, do not believe it. While there are several individuals who have attained the direct experience of oneness, they do not make such claims. They rely on the perceptions of those around them to discern their true estate. It can be felt. There are deceivers in your midst that use words to say some very intriguing things, but you cannot FEEL their connection with Source the way you can with those who are really in that state. Trust what you FEEL. Your feelings are a better indicator of truth than your minds, which can be led off in many directions, pursuing this theory or that, but which are disconnected from the direct EXPERIENCE of truth.

We began our discussion today with the statement that we would address the experiences you are having as the cleansing proceeds. We told you our little story to give these next remarks a proper context. Please bear with us if we are unusually long-winded today, for this is not an easy thing to convey.

Each of you has been like Thimble, feeling lost and alone in the vast world around you, and wanting to get back to the world of your dreams without knowing how to get there. Eventually, you began to reach out to the Great Thimble-maker and ask for Its help. Your request has been heard, and now you are being lifted—not by a beautiful white bird (although that is a common symbol for Spirit)—but by a vibrational shift. Picture for a moment a large, sea-going vessel. It has been sailing the ocean for a long time, and its bottom is covered with seaweed and barnacles and slime. Now the vessel has been taken up into drydock and all of the things that were clinging to its underside are being cleaned off, in preparation for another voyage in another sea. This is what is happening to you.

All of the things that have become attached to you are being cleaned off. You are shedding the emotional charges that have been accumulated through the entire course of your embodied journey through the history of this planet, so you are re-experiencing many emotions that have been dormant in your cellular memory and are now rising to the surface. You are having the barnacles removed from your eyes, and you are beginning to see with more clarity. You are experiencing completions with those whom you have traveled with, so that you will be totally free of all attachments that would keep you from being your essential self. You are not aware yet of just how those attachments have bound you to this Earth, but as they pass from your life and you begin to be free of them, you will realize the subtle hold they had on you and how they limited you in your expression of your true essence.

All of these things are now passing out of you and out of your lives, including the IDEAS you had about what was true, about what your "true nature" looks like. You are probably feeling LESS tolerant of what you see around you, in spite of your "pictures" of what a "light worker" is supposed to be like. You are increasing in your ability to forgive and to have compassion at the very same time you are feeling more judgmental and critical of the abuses of power you see all around you, but remember that those in power got there through the collective consent of all who contributed to their being there. Now that the door is closed on the probabilities and the course is set, many are waking up to the painful realization that there are consequences to all actions—both those that do things and those that do not do things. Those who sat by, content to let others do their thinking for them, are having an unpleasant awakening to the consequences of that action. INACTION is also action, you see. The entire process that is unfolding now on the planet will expose the underbelly of the "ship of state," as it were, and the "creatures" that have been hidden on that underbelly will be seen more and more openly as the days proceed toward the conclusion.

This is all part of the process of the planet completing with this level of her being, and because she is like your own child, you feel anger, rage, and perhaps impotence at what you see going on. Those of you who don't like feeling impotent are feeling either desperation or determination to DO SOMETHING, depending on the degree of powerlessness or empowerment you have achieved, but it all comes down to the same thing. This final desecration WILL play out, and it has as its purpose the experience of the desecration and the suffering that will result from it. It is easy to blame the Creator and be angry about the suffering, but how else can the "lesson" be taught? The greater mass of people will not get the "lesson" with less drastic means. They would rather stay asleep and let someone else do their thinking for them, so they need a "rude awakening," not unlike Thimble in our story. The purpose of the awakening is to set one's heart and mind toward seeking in the right direction—toward the Great Thimble-maker—for solutions. The cause of everything you see that is "wrong" with the way people conduct themselves on the planet—including their reproductive behavior—is a lack of connection with Source. To make the connection with Source, one must first perceive the need for that connection. As long as one's material needs are the primary object, one is not very inclined to seek a higher Source. So the material underpinnings will be stripped away from many and placed in the hands of the few, and the suffering of the many will increase. In fact, that is already well along in the process.

You who are reading this are the pioneers. You have begun your awakening a little ahead of the rest. You have begun reaching toward Source a little sooner than the great mass of humanity, and you will come back to lead to safety those who have needed their lessons from what lies ahead for this planet and everything upon it.

The animals, plants, and other "innocents" in this drama will go on to live on other planets, and you suffer when you see their suffering because of your great love for this planet and all of her lifeforms—including the rocks, the rivers, the skies, the air, and the plants and animals who have been so impacted by human actions. You are going to return to the land of your dreams, and you are being cleansed of everything that would keep you bound to this plane and level of reality. You are acting like lightning rods to ground the higher light into the atomic structure of the planet, and your bodies are going though many changes as a result of this function that you perform, not all of which are pleasant and some of which can be quite frightening because you do not feel in control.

The best "medicine" we can prescribe for all the "ills" of these changes is to increase your depth of SURRENDER. Turn all of these things over to God (however you conceive of It), and deepen your connection to Source. Deepen your trust in the journey, and surrender up all resistance to what you see going on around you and within you. Surrender up your fears, also. When you do not feel in control, fear rises to your awareness. Let the fear come, and then sit with it. Let it percolate through you and move out of you and observe it. Observe that the fear can be within you and you are not obliterated by it. Observe that you do not have to be controlled by your fear. If you feel yourself "losing it" and becoming paralyzed by your fear, remember your connection to Source and use that as the thing that you cling to, rather than your attachment to a particular outcome. All of your fears, all of your suffering and pain has some measure of attachment to a particular outcome or course of events. It all is a form of resistance to the movement of life, especially now, in these accelerated times.

We have said it before and we will say it again. "Let go and let God handle the details." You are shedding all of the debris you have acquired during your many lives on the face of this planet. It is not comfortable at times, but remember that you are losing only that which is not part of your essential self. You are being cleaned of all the barnacles and slime that you have taken on in your voyage through this ocean, and will be lifted into "drydock" to complete the process. Then you will be all clean and shiny and new, and will embark on other journeys in other seas, for this Earth and this sea will have passed away and be there no more.

Amen, Adonoy Sabayoth. We are the Hosts of Heaven. We love you. We are with you. You are one OF us and you are one WITH us, and you are awakening to that truth now. We leave you now, in peace and honor and blessing. We shall speak to you again.

ON SEXUALITY AND REPRODUCTION— TERRA STYLE
April 14, 2001

Well, now. In our last conversation, we spoke to you about the one-ness that you will experience on Terra. This will be your constant experience, and you will KNOW yourself as being part of everything you perceive—be it infinitesimally small or as vast as an entire universe. Therefore, the primary reason for the 3D human sexual behavior will not be present. What IS the primary reason for your sexual behavior? When analyzed down to its root, it is primarily an attempt to escape the prison of being contained in one body, of seeking to somehow breach that boundary of skin and to attempt to merge with another. Now, we are aware that many times the sexual act is not used to JOIN two people, so much as it is the inflicting of one's power over another, but that is a distortion and misappropriation of the sexual energy, as you will soon see.

Rather than condemn the present patterns, we wish to first draw a picture for you of how it will be on Terra—not only for the human species, but for all life forms that have the ability to join in sexual ways. Then, by contrast, you will be able to gain a sense of how your present experience does not satisfy and provides only temporary relief from your isolation and separation from all things. You will also see how those practices that seek to escape from the sexual function, such as celibacy and monasticism, are an evasion of life in its fullest expression. That is not to say that there is nothing to be gained by them, but we prefer to put before you what life is like when you are in full consciousness and not struggling to repress your natural, God-given faculties in order to transcend them.

So, let us begin this discussion by reminding you that on Terra, you will be in total oneness with all of Creation. You will be immersed in a sea of consciousness that from your present perspective would appear to be surreal and dreamlike—not unlike some of the states one experiences on certain drugs, such as opium and its relatives. However, it will be your constant state, and therefore one simply adapts to it as being the norm and picks up from there. On Terra, all things are in total balance with the whole, and reproduction occurs within that context. No flower blooms, no animal is born, without there being a clear and necessary "reason" for its coming into being, with regard to the whole. All things that reproduce by the combining of gametes (sperm and ova in their various forms) only do so when the whole demands it of them, in order to perpetuate and maintain the balance. It sounds very complicated, but we assure you that it is the only truly natural way for it to be. What you see in your present reality is so distorted from what is natural that you cannot imagine what "natural" (i.e. in keeping with the inherent NATURE of things) is really like.

On Terra, reproduction is one function and it is separate from the sexual function. In your present reality, they are so intertwined and so out of balance with Nature and what is natural that they are often confused for one another. In many of your religions, both desire and sexuality are feared and held in mistrust. You are taught that they are something "sinful" or "wild" or "uncivilized" that has to be controlled in one way or another. However, when a natural function is repressed, just like when the flow of a stream is blocked, it WILL seek another outlet, and that is exactly what you see in your present world. The natural functions have become twisted and distorted and grossly misunderstood in every aspect of your present civilization, regardless of geography or so-called "enlightened" approaches to the problem, which is really a symptom of the experience of separation.

On Terra, you will be one with everyone and everything, all the way out into the far reaches of the cosmos. You will live on a world in which everything is in total balance and shares in the existence and consciousness of everything else. If you are already in full union with everything, where does desire fit into the picture? Desire is the engine behind all creativity, be it to create a painting, a piece of music, an elegant mathematical equation, or to create another life. Desire is what drives the evolution of the cosmos. The Creator's desire to experience everything is what leads It to CREATE everything!

At its root, your desire is the outpicturing of the Creator's desire to experience everything, through the mechanism of the interaction of all the parts of Its Creation. This interaction is most acutely experienced through the faculty of touch. You can look at something and interact with it visually. You can share your thoughts and feelings with another, either verbally or telepathically. You can experience through your physical senses of hearing and smell, but none of these communicates experience as fully as the sense of touch. You can use your imagination to create an experience that approaches what it would be like to touch something, but there really is no substitute for the actual touching. In order to progress to the higher levels of being, one must complete with the levels below it. Although you are the embodied aspects of the Elohim and have DESCENDED into matter, you still can only imagine the "next step" on the journey back to Source in terms of your present experience—that of a human being, clothed in skin, and seeking to break out of the prison of separation consciousness. Therefore, you can only imagine a "next step," and that is how we will frame this. In a future discussion, we will talk about how you aren't really "going" anywhere, but for now, let us continue the exploration of our topic today.

The sense of touch is where you, as human beings, are most starved. And yet, if you seek to touch from that place of hunger and not from a place of already being filled with love, you only perpetuate your distress, and you get caught up in either having to seek again or remain in the loneliness and isolation of your prison cell—your physical body, your container—the thimble that you wear around the fingertip of your Oversoul that is inserted into your present time-space locus. Let that sink in for a moment, and let that awareness of all the lives in which you sought to fill your emptiness and were unfulfilled in your seeking come back to you now. Let it sink in, and let it go. That is all coming to an end for you now.

On Terra, every life form that reproduces by sexual means is mated. Every life form in that category is paired with its twin—its counterpart—what we call the dyad. Each Oversoul is complete within itself, just as the Creator is complete within Itself. There is no division into parts or genders, but in Its desire to experience everything, the Creator divided Itself into many parts that could then seek to unify back together again, and then—having accomplished that—would be divided up into an entirely new Creation—what could be viewed as the exhale and the inhale of the Creator's breath. First the exhalation—the breathing out into form, and then the inhalation—the coalescing of form back into the formlessness that gave rise to it in the first place. The dyad is really the first level of the Creator (the monad) dividing itself into parts. This happens at all levels of the Creation, but for now we will keep our focus on the most apparent form of that—the twin, the counterpart that is the "other part" that each part seeks to find and unify with. We will call this part the "mate" of the other.

Mating is not just for reproduction. Mating is the act of unifying with one's mate, and reproduction is reserved for those times when a new being or unit is required for the balance of the whole. Population levels on Terra will remain fairly stable, once the colonization is complete. It will take some time to accomplish that, but once it is complete, those forms that leave Terra in one way or another will be replaced by others, and thereby maintain the balance of the whole. As humans, you will have very long lifespans and be capable of reproducing throughout your entire adult existence. Therefore, in order to maintain the proper reproductive rate, gametes (sperms and ova) will only be produced when there is the complete set of circumstances present that require the creation of another life form. That is "birth control" in its natural form, at the highest level of knowing. We will address the issue of birthing in another conversation, but for now let us return to our topic for today.

The bodies you now occupy are not the bodies you will have

on Terra. The bodies you now occupy will transform into the kind of body that you would consider one of a god or goddess, because of its physical perfection and beauty. The physical senses you now have are very crude compared to those you will have then. Just as you cannot make a fine drawing with a pencil that is shaped like a log, you cannot experience the fineness of sensuality that will be available to you on Terra with the coarseness of your present physical senses. Note the relationship between sensuality and senses. Just as sexuality is the expression of the sexual function, sensuality is the expression of the sensual (pertaining to the senses) function. Sensuality is intertwined with sexuality because sexuality involves the senses for its proper expression.

All of the senses are engaged in the sexual function, both the physical ones and the ones you would call "subtle"—your intuitive, mental, and emotional ones. Those of you who have been fortunate enough to have a glimpse of a full sexual experience know this, but unfortunately that is the exception rather than the rule, and just as your cultures have labeled sexuality as something to be feared and controlled, sensuality has likewise been condemned to repression and condemnation. On Terra, you will be freed of all constraints—especially economic ones—and you will be in full consciousness, blessed with lives measured in the hundreds of years, so you will be able to allow yourself the full expression of all of your senses and your sexuality, in a mated relationship, without any reproductive consequences.

You won't need techniques. You won't need anything but the full acceptance of your freedom to endlessly explore the full range of your sensuality—ALL of your senses—and your desire will be finally free to explore creativity of all kinds of things, without being confined by "rules" as to what is acceptable and what is not. In full consciousness at all times, you will KNOW and intuitively seek only those expressions that support and celebrate life and support and celebrate the whole of life, in its myriad of forms and expressions. Ecstasy is your natural estate, difficult as that might be to comprehend from your present frame of reference, and the sexual function—employing the full range of all of your senses as it does—will give you the greatest fulfillment of that ecstasy, and so it will occupy your attention a great deal of the time. When you are in continuous communication with all of Creation, and in particular with your mate—the other side of your dyadic unit—it will be like "making love" all of the time. Even when you are not in physical proximity, you will be making love with each other. The flow is constant between you, like a dance that never ends, and it will be so for the rest of your journey in this Creation.

You were born together in the mind of the Creator, you are joined together in the mind of the Creator, and you will eternally be together in the mind of the Creator until the inhale is complete and you dissolve your beingness into that of the Creator Itself, ready to be born again into beingness with the next outbreath of Creation. You have much ahead to enjoy, and enjoy it you will, of that we have no doubt. It is time, dear ones, for you to come home—to yourself, to Terra, to the entire spectrum of experience of which you are capable. And is THAT not an idea worth waiting for! WE think so, and know you will agree.

We will leave you now in peace and honor and blessing. Amen, Adonoy Sabayoth. We are the Hosts of Heaven. We shall speak to you again.

ACROSS THE GREAT DIVIDE
September 1, 2001

We have asked to speak to you today about the next stage on the journey to Terra, and to address a central question that is no doubt at the back of your minds as you read through our communications with you. How, exactly, will you cross over the gulf between your present physical location and your future home on Terra? And what exactly are these ships that we talk about so often in so many ways?

To begin with, our ships are made of living light. They are conscious beings in their own right, and come into being without being "manufactured" via some technology or machinery in a factory. They are precipitated directly from the matrix of being that we call the Creator. They are sentient and we travel in them by forming a telepathic link between ourselves and the ship we are on, and together—as a group mind—we teleport ourselves to the agreed-upon location. We travel in what you refer to as hyperspace. We "blink off" from one location and "blink on" in the place we project ourselves into. The ship acts as a container for our bodies, which are still physical to us, even though they would not be visible to instruments or organs that are tuned to the light frequencies that you are familiar with as your present physical environment.

These ships all have names, just as we do. They have personalities, just as we do. They come into being in response to a collective need for their presence, just as all forms do on Terra and in the frequency band that we occupy. As we said in our last Message, no form comes into being on Terra except as it is in harmony with the whole. The whole would be incomplete without it, and that lack is filled by the manifestation of the ship or any other form that appears in that frequency band. All are in conscious communion with the Creator, with each other, and with the planet, through the vehicle of a group mind. Each being within the group mind has its own perspective and makes it possible for anyone else in the group to experience through that perspective if that is desired, but most of the time we are content to remain in our own "viewing chamber," as we are always filled and never lack for anything. The spontaneous desires that emerge in our minds source from the Creator and lead us in the direction that fulfills Divine Will at all times. Everything is always aligned with Divine Will and therefore we are always filled with a sense of unspeakable joy and fullness, as we just live the "rightness" of our being as a permanent way of doing things.

So, when we say we will come for you in our beautiful ships, it is a group effort. We and the ships are united in our purpose and being, and the radiance of that can be felt by those who can join their energies with ours and therefore become part of the group and join with us in our location. Think about this for a moment. You probably thought we were going to use some sort of beam or technology to lift you into the ships, but we don't do the lifting. YOU do! It is through the energy of joy in your heart—the welcome you feel in seeing us—that the doors fly open and you naturally gravitate (or should we say, "levitate"?) to the fulfillment of your heart's desire.

As we have said, love is the ordering force that acts upon light to create all form. It acts in opposition to entropy, which seeks to return things to a more elemental, uncreated state. Love is the life force behind everything and those who understand the nature of healing know that love is the most powerful healing force there is. It mends those places where entropy has torn the connections, where you are wounded in your bodies and in your psyches. A wound is only a tear in the fabric of life. Love is the force that mends the tear. We have asked you to face down your fears so that you can hold more love in your hearts. When it is time for the lifting, you will be ready and your own love and joy will be the force that reunites you with your spiritual family.

Now we would like to address another part of the "project"— namely how you get from Earth to Terra. As we have said, the planet will undergo a total cleansing of all life above the mineral kingdom, in order to lie fallow and regenerate the physical body of Earth itself. It will withdraw from a state where it can support life and reappear in its new body, somewhat like a glove being turned inside out to reveal a new "outside" that was formerly hidden from sight. This inversion will take place over a period of several years and no life forms will inhabit the former planet during that time. It is necessary to lift some life forms off of the planet before the completion of the final cataclysms and to house and provide for them while the planet completes her own transition from one form to another. This is where the ships come in.

Our ships are not just modes of transportation. They are like floating wombs and can support us and all life forms within them- selves, like giant islands or capsules in the vastness of space. The very large motherships are spherical in shape, due to the properties that are inherent in a sphere. You will all be joining us on board our smaller, disc-shaped craft and then be transported to an enormous mothership that is nearly the size of your own planet, but not quite so large—on the order of 80% of your present planet's size. You will live with us on board the mothership until all preparations are complete and then you will be transported to Terra to set up your homes there. You will undergo a process while on board the mothership that will raise your consciousness to the point of full union with the Creator and it will remain that way for the rest of your existence in the higher densities. None of you who are going to Terra will ever have to return to a 3D existence, although you might at some time choose to do that for your own reasons, in keeping with the purpose of your existence as an individuated part of the consciousness of the whole.

Now the process has indeed begun in earnest. "Launch day" for Operation Terra (August 18, 2001) marked the departure and separating out of that group of beings and that envelope of energy that is headed toward Terra from the mass consciousness and body of Earth. So, in a way, you are already being "lifted" and you are already taking part in your homecoming and reunion with your soul family. The Earth-based portion of Operation Terra is a focal point, a gathering place for all those who are destined for Terra. Many of you have been in total isolation from others like yourselves, and that isolation is beginning to end as you discover that you are not the only one who knows what you know and feels as you feel. Operation Terra is a beacon with the tone of "home" to those who resonate with this information. Note that we do not say "agree with" or "believe in" this information. We use the word resonance on purpose, because it says exactly what we mean.

If you look at the word resonance, it comes from the root "resound," or literally to re-sound, or "sound again." It is a form of echo, sending back (re-sounding) the sound that triggered it in the first place. Sound is measured in frequency patterns and the interaction of sound and light combined make up the basis of all form. We have embedded light codes into the Operation Terra material, using the words as the carrier wave to bring them into your awareness. As you read the words, the light codes pass into your body and seek the matching codes in your cellular structure. It is very much like a tuning fork. If you are a tuning fork, tuned to the note "A," nothing will happen until a note "A" is struck or sounded in your vicinity. Then you will re-sound (resound) with that note, and it will ring inside you like a bell, an explosion of sound and joy as your embedded codes begin making their own sound in response. It might be a quiet sound. It might be like a light-cannon going off, but it will feel like a "yes." "Yes, I know this." "Yes, this is familiar to me." "Yes, this is mine." That is how resonance works. It is not the product of analytical thought. It is a RESPONSE, a resonance, a re-sounding and answering echo from the core of your being, your own inner answer to the question, "Has it happened"? "Has it shown up yet?"

Yes, we have shown up now. And you belong with us, your soul family. You are drawn through the principle of resonance to recognize this note as yours. Now the "lifting" can be seen as a logical outgrowth of that—an extension of that resonance with our note, as it is carried through this information and the light codes we put into it. Now it is not so mysterious, not so much a "beam me up, Scotty" hardware-based technology. Call it the technology of love. Call it the technology of the life force. Can you feel your heart and being opening to this idea like the petals of a flower spreading to catch the rays of the sun? We are here with you at all times, and we welcome you into our midst. Our love for you showers you at all times, like the sun is always radiating light toward the Earth, and all you have to do is open yourself to receive it.

It will be easier for you if you do not engage with the pictures that are playing out on the perceptual screen of the rest of the world as things proceed. If you detach from all of that, you will find you experience more peace, more bliss, and more serene acceptance of yourselves and your journey. If you over-identify with what you look upon—the apparent suffering that is increasing, the madness playing out around you—it is easy for you to forget your home note—the joy and the peace and the love that you feel when you connect with us and our vibration. So, if you find yourself getting caught up in the storm, in the battles that are raging even now and that will only escalate as things proceed toward the climax, when you become aware of how uncomfortable you feel in that frequency band, just disengage. Come back to the Messages. Read them again. Go for a walk. Let yourself register that most of what you see around you is not yours. Let the beauty show itself to you, peeking out from behind the ugliness. It is there. Let yourself open to it. Disengage. Let it all go. Let go and let God handle the details.

You are tired at times. Let yourself rest in the peace and the joy and the love. It is there for you, if you can let yourself receive it. Let yourself receive it. Let go of everything that does not bring you peace and joy and love. Sleep deeply and gratefully when you rest, and let us scour you clean of the residue that remains. You may be tired afterward, but you will feel much lighter and freer because of the work we are doing with you while you sleep. Let go and let God. It is much easier that way.

We leave you now, in peace and honor and blessing. We shall speak to you again.

Amen, Adonoy Sabayoth. We are the Hosts of Heaven.

"The ingathering will remove all but a few of you from the planetary surface. Some will remain because their work for the planet requires it, but most of you will be lifted up out of the frequency band you now occupy and be totally hidden away until it is time to return. You will not be available to those who are left behind, so that they may have their opportunity to learn what you have learned. It is all in divine order and all within the Divine Plan."

THE TIME OF INGATHERING
September 8, 2001

Today we would like to talk to you about some of the things that are about to begin showing up on your perceptual screen. We would remind you to keep your breath open, as some of the things we will be talking about may cause some temporary discomfort to contemplate. We would prefer to not ever cause you any discomfort, but sometimes during a birth, there is some pain and pressure, and the more you can simply accept the process—in all of its aspects—the easier the process will go for you.

That being said, you—as a planetary population—are about to enter a time of deepening strife and travail. There is safe haven within yourself, no matter where you are located on the planetary surface, and we are close at hand, guiding and protecting and showering our love and grace over you. Whatever we may say here, whatever your eyes may see as you look around you, please remember that. If you feel yourself being overwhelmed by anything, just close your eyes for a moment, deepen your breathing, and come into your center. Feel the ground beneath your feet and remain rooted there until you are calm and serene in the midst of everything.

The first symptoms of the unraveling have begun to appear. The first wobbles of the axis are occurring and the center of things has begun to oscillate between one pole and another—both geophysically, politically, economically, and culturally. There is a profound change underway that affects every aspect of life in every part of the world, and all parts interact with and are connected to every other part, so the change will oscillate and ramify and be amplified with each oscillation. This is part of the "shaking" that we have talked about, and it will shake loose everything before it is over. Nothing of the old ways will pass through this time. Only essence will survive and move on. Only what is in keeping with YOUR essence will survive the shift and move on. Many of the acculturated patterns will not make it through the "gate," and you will truly become entirely new beings.

On the way to the homecoming, though, you will pass through scenes of increasing turmoil and chaos. Many will be very frightened, as the fabric of their life becomes torn and shattered through these massive shifts and changes in the foundation that underlies the entire system. However, this is what their Oversouls chose for them to experience in this life, and it is also a time that is rich with opportunity for discovering what is REALLY important, for discovering where one's priorities really lie. It will not be an easy time, but as so many of you have already discovered by going through your own travail, there is something gained in the end that is more precious than any material possession could possibly be. It is the inner peace and release that comes from surrender that is the "gold" within the cloud. It is the golden treasure of Spirit that will fill you now, and it is the time of the ingathering.

This will not be an easy thing for some of you to hear, because you care and you want to help and you still have fears about what will happen to the "others." Even so, this is as it was intended to be from the beginning, and is totally in keeping with the choices made by all of the Oversouls, individually and collectively. The ingathering is taking place now, and it represents the collecting of those who are going to Terra and removing them from the world scene for a time, until it is time to return and gather up those who have gone through the trials and been transformed by them.

This is about the harvest, and if we may take a few lines from your Bible, it is the time to separate the wheat from the tares, to send the workers into the fields and gather it into the barns. This is the time of the ingathering, and the withdrawal from the world for a time, until it is time to return. Let this sink in. Let this register. Let it fill you and let it deepen you and let it flow, without resistance, until you are at peace. Let all the resistance come up and move out of you. Let it all go. Let go and let God. Let go. Breathe. Breathe. Breathe.

There is no more to be done than to gather up those who are being lifted now. Then the full impact of the travail of the birth will play out on the planetary surface, and there will be much pain and suffering wherever there is resistance. This is a mighty, scouring force, and it will not be pleasant for many who go through it, but it must occur. The lesson is one of surrender and of turning inward for support and succor. There are some lessons to be learned about the consequences of not taking responsibility for one's life and truth. There are some lessons to be learned about abdicating responsibility for one's life and truth and placing it into the hands of others. There will be many hard lessons learned.

The ingathering will remove all but a few of you from the planetary surface. Some will remain because their work for the planet requires it, but most of you will be lifted up out of the frequency band you now occupy and be totally hidden away until it is time to return. You will not be available to those who are left behind, so that they may have their opportunity to learn what you have learned. It is all in divine order and all within the Divine Plan. You are already being lifted now, and that separating out from the mass consciousness can be felt by those of you who are sufficiently sensitive to the more subtle energies to perceive it.

It will appear that the light is withdrawn with you, but that will never be the case. It will appear that you have abandoned those who remain behind, but that will never be the case. You will simply be withdrawing for a time so that you can return to help when you are really needed. You need to change your costume for your new role, and you need a safe place in which to accomplish that. You are simply going away to prepare for the real help you can give, and you will be needed in great numbers near the end of things, as there will be many who need your help at that time. The kind of help you can give now is fairly limited, although your task of grounding the light and your meditation and prayers have been very effective in supporting the cleansing so far. But when it comes time to gather up those who have gone through the time of trials, it will not be enough to offer words of comfort or a book to read or a meditation circle. By then, things will be very different than they are now and a different kind of help will be needed. Wars and climate change and economic collapse and tyranny will all have taken their toll, and simple techniques and words will not be enough. You will literally walk through the killing fields and offer a hand to those who are ready to leave with you. You will need to be clothed in your armor of protection and you will need to be in full consciousness. You will be as living Christs (anointed ones) and carry the vibration and power that comes through such a state of being.

So now the lifting proceeds and the separating out proceeds and all will play out in increasingly serious fashion. You will find that, even though all is collapsing around you, you will have peace. You will have peace because you will have learned the lessons and will have learned how to surrender to the higher light and wisdom. You will have peace because you have learned how to face down your fears and accept your life's path with serenity. In that peace, you will find bliss and relief and you will accept the light and the lifting. So, now, let go of the feeling that there is anything to do now but accept the lifting. The things that will play out on the planetary surface MUST play out and there is nothing you need to resist or change. Let go and let God, and receive the peace of that.

Let peace be your refuge and armor against the pain of those around you. You cannot help them if you engage in their pain. You cannot be lifted if you are still clinging to the old forms and patterns. Let go and let God. Let God handle the details. You are not responsible for anyone but yourself. It is enough to receive the lifting, for by that means you will be able to really help when it is needed. We have been repeating ourselves throughout this Message because we really want you to "get it." Let go and let God. Do not resist what is happening around you. Receive peace.

All your life, and in all of your lives, you have been preparing for this time. It is here now. If you had a feeling that you had to DO something—set up a center, found a movement, teach a class, write a book—for most of you, that time is now over. For SOME of you—those who have elected to remain behind and who have work to do through the difficult times ahead—you will be guided and you will know what is yours to do. Each one of you reading this has a part to play in all of this. Some of you will remain and play your part that way for now; the rest will be lifted gradually until you are "gone from the scene," so that you can complete your "costume change" and prepare for your new role. We are with you all, and we will be coming closer to you now, so many of you who have not felt us will be able to feel us now. You have been activated by the light codes in these Messages and it is easier now for you to receive us. Let go and let God. Let go of your attachments as to how it will be for you or for those around you. Let it all be the way it is intended to be and you will have joy in all your undertakings. There will come a time when it is all ended, and then you will have Terra to look forward to. Let go. Float upwards. Let go. We are with you, every step of the way.

We leave you now in peace and honor and blessing. Amen, Adonoy Sabayoth. We are the Hosts of Heaven.

"Each of you who is attuned to these
Messages is being stimulated to emit
a particular frequency pattern, and as
more and more of you join in with your
"notes," the collective energies and patterns
will build in strength until they shatter the frequency
envelope—the "glass ceiling"—that surrounds the
planet. You will be shattering the energetic patterns
of the existing paradigm, and opening the pathway
for the emergence of a totally new world to emerge
from this one."

SHATTERING GLASS

September 14, 2001

All right, now. The first "bomb" has been dropped and the cloud of the aftermath is billowing forth across the entire planet. How does this fit in with the overall plan? How is one to be with the scenes of horror and pain? How can one bear the load of believing in truth, kindness, and love in the face of such an act and the pain it inflicts?

Dear ones, we know your hearts are heavy and saddened by such scenes on your perceptual screens. We know you are sympathetic with those impulses toward goodness, beauty and mercy. We know you deeply care for this planet and all upon it, as we do. Therefore, we would offer the following as our contribution toward your process of coming to grips with that which is now unfolding upon your planet, and to further the deepening of your awareness of just what that is and what it will require of you.

You have incarnated here at this time to perform a very special and difficult task, in service to the planet (and secondarily to all upon her). Your focus is the planet, and the assistance you can give to the planet as she begins rising toward her new form and being as Terra. You are assistants in the birthing of this new world, and once this "launch phase" is complete, you will withdraw from her for a time until the trajectory is complete and she has arrived and manifested in her new state. At that time, all that were taken off the planet for this particular purpose will become the architects of the new society, the gardeners of the new garden, Terra. Please note that there are many other destinations and we are addressing our remarks to those who have this special task. They do not apply to anyone else at this time.

As we have said before, you are human lightning rods, grounding the higher light into the core of the planet. This light is a cleansing light, and is aiding the planet in shedding all those thoughtforms that she has absorbed over the course of her history as the host for all of the lifeforms that have come forth upon her surface. As the planet rises through the frequency bands, all of those thoughtforms that she contains will be cast off, largely through the force of the light being beamed down into the planet from the higher realms—through your sun, through the galactic core, and through each of you. You are each supporting the cleansing of the planet, and the scenes you witness (such as what just occurred) are the outpicturing of those thoughtforms that are being flushed to the surface—pictures of hatred for others to such a degree it seeks to annihilate them and cause them every conceivable harm—personal, economic, humiliation, and so forth.

You have a saying, "What goes around, comes around." Some of you are also aware of the concept of karma—that whatever action proceeds from a place of imbalance must be balanced by an equal and opposite action of some kind. What you may NOT be aware of is that there is an invisible wall—a threshold that separates your present Creation from the Creation that is about to be birthed, on the other side of the "blink."

Your planet is moving upward in frequency and forward in time, as viewed from within linear time. It is approaching this barrier, this threshold, and all actions that source from imbalance will receive their answering action, like an echo bouncing off that barrier and returning to the source of the imbalanced energies, as a correction and offset to those actions. The Earth is ascending now, and can no longer absorb these things, as she has throughout her history. What this means is that two things will be going on simultaneously, and will tend to amplify one another as things proceed.

First, there is the shedding of the thoughtforms of previous actions, from other times in the Earth's history. All of those thought-forms that are not in keeping with the higher frequency bands will surface and be re-enacted in a present time context, so they can be experienced and balanced by those who are ready to receive them as that kind of opportunity—who are ready to shift their own historical response to another kind of response, one based on mercy, love, kindness, compassion, and unifying with those whom they previously opposed. The second thing that will be going on will be the echoes of present-time actions, the answering actions that mirror and reflect the initial actions, so that the sources of those actions have an opportunity to shift their response to a different kind of response, also.

Both of these things—the echoes from the past and the echoes from the present—will be going on simultaneously, which will intensify and multiply the effects as the planet moves upward and forward towards its own destination. How this will be experienced by each "observer"—each set of eyes and ears that are present to witness this—will vary, according to the "filters" that are in place in that individual. So some will see things that they feel called upon to avenge. Others will see things that they feel called upon to heal. Still others will respond in other ways. It is all a very individual thing, so that the Creator can experience Itself through all the perspectives available through all of Its creations. We would remind you that nothing exists that is not part of and contained within the Creator, and the greatest comfort is obtained by making that connection with the Creator and aligning one's personal will with the Creator's will. "Not my will, but thy will" is the way it was said 2,000 years ago, and it is still valid now.

So what does this mean at a practical level, and what is your proper response and most appropriate service, given the above? First of all, you must understand and come to terms with the enormity of what is unfolding. Consider that you are dealing with the outpicturing of ALL ACTIONS that occurred throughout the entire history of the planet, up to and including those actions that are arising in present time. That is the size of the burden that the planet has carried as her service to those upon her, so that maximum opportunities for experience could occur. We are talking about the compression of millions and BILLIONS of years' worth of events into the span of your present time, which will complete in a few years from now. Take a breath and let the scope of that register deeply within you, as you receive the confirmation of what you already know to be true.

There is some relief in this picture, given that most of the imbalance has sourced from the most recent periods of history, and that some of the actions that arise in the present are in themselves echoes from prior periods, being revisited in your present time, so you might say that there is some inherent efficiency in this process, as present actions can act to correct and balance prior ones at the same time as they are corrected and balanced. Nonetheless, the burden of the planet is enormous, the timespan is relatively short, and so the potential intensity of the process is almost inconceivable, if you could indeed grasp it at all.

But there is help being given in enormous quantities, also. Those of you who are embodied on the planet's surface are the point of entry for the forces of Love and Grace that are being showered down by those in the higher realms. The core of the Andromeda Galaxy (which overlights your galaxy), the Great Central Sun of your galaxy, and your own sun are all acting as lenses to step down the Light from Source and to make it available to those of you who serve on the planet's surface at this time, in amounts and "packets" that you can handle without being destroyed by their intensity and power. So your task is to allow yourselves to receive these energies and to let them flow through you unimpeded, into the planet's core. The more you can surrender your own resistance to the process and simply allow yourselves to become like hollow tubes through which the flow can pass, the more you can contribute to this process. This will also allow you to remain calm, serene, and centered while all around you is in chaos. If you allow yourselves to be used in this way, you will be promoting the highest good for ALL involved—all of the players in all of the dramas, and most of all, the planet herself.

So as you look upon each succeeding wave of change as it unfurls, you must also understand that beneath the terrible scenes, there is a great healing taking place. The fact that these issues were not dealt with in the past has only created a greater pressure for them to be dealt with now. None of you can say you have not contributed in some way to what you are witnessing now. You are all part of and intimately connected to these actions through your interconnectedness with each other, with the economic systems, and with all life on the planet. This is the deep level of understanding that is necessary for you to grasp, in order to serve this task. You must surrender up all feelings of guilt and unworthiness to aid in this service. Each of you has played the parts that were selected by your Oversouls across all of your embodiments, and all of those were chosen in harmony with the Creator's own desire to experience everything. That desire on the part of the Creator was the impulse that led to the Creation in the first place, so one must surrender to the entirety of the experience—to become large enough to hold it all within oneself, just as the Creator does.

You have all been stretched to grow in different ways in the past, but now it takes on a different face. Now you must stretch to become big enough to contain it all within yourself. This is what it means to be a Master. If you get stuck in pictures of "us and them," you are only perpetuating separation. As difficult as it may seem to attain, you must come to the place of being able to look upon all of these actions as if you yourself had authored them, because in truth, if you pursue things to their core, it is always the Creator Itself that you will find at the core, so the "true you" IS the Creator and therefore this IS your Creation, in some sense. There really isn't anything else BUT the Creator, and in time, you will have this as your complete and unending, direct experience, and then you will also have permanent peace and joy. You must each find your way to this understanding in your own way and your own time. However, if you can create a sanctuary for yourself within yourself, and deliberately choose to go into that inner sanctuary whenever these assaults upon your sensitivities occur, you will be allowing that which needs to move to move, and you will be able to remain sane and peaceful in the midst of it all. If you engage with the scenes around you and identify with them, you will be swept into the chaos and be overwhelmed by the enormity of what you perceive, to the point of hopelessness and despair if you persist in that behavior. Instead, we urge you to go within, to detach, and thereby hold the truth of the center—the calm eye in the center of the storm.

We have called this Message, "Shattering Glass" for a reason. Each of you who is connecting with the vision and vibration of Terra is emitting a sound—your particular frequency pattern in the matrix of sound that underlies the material universe. As you attune to the light codes carried in these Messages, you will re-sound them back into the universe, amplifying them and uniting them with the "broadcasts" sent up by your fellow workers who are sharing this task with you. As more and more of you find your way to these Messages and are activated by the light codes, more and more of your frequency patterns will be available to do the necessary work.

You have a phrase—"the glass ceiling." It is most often used to depict an invisible barrier to upward movement on a career path, but we are borrowing this concept now to refer to another kind of glass ceiling—an invisible frequency barrier that has surrounded this planet and kept things contained within her and cycling over and over upon her surface throughout her history as a planet—an invisible barrier that must be breached in order for the planet to move upward in her own ascension path—her own "career path." When a baby is in the womb, it is encased in a membrane or sac. When it is time for the birth, the membrane splits so that the baby can come forth unfettered and begin its new life as a new being, independent of those tissues that nourished it and protected it throughout its time in the womb.

Just so, the Earth is enclosed in a frequency barrier, similar to a membrane, that must be breached or split, in order for her to come forth and begin her new life. The barrier is a container for the present experience and it must be shattered to allow movement to a new experience. Each of you is emitting a sound pattern. All of your sound patterns are beginning to converge and join together into a larger pattern, becoming amplified where you have particular frequencies that match those of the others in the group. As your own frequencies rise, the collective frequency of the group will also rise, and the sound that you emit will grow in volume, louder and louder as more and more of you are attuned by these Messages and their light codes. We are giving you the "keys" that unlock your own codings, and through these Messages, we are "tuning" your own "transmitters"—the living light crystals at the core of your cellular memory that send forth your own frequency pattern. As your individual transmissions combine with those of your group, they will amplify and rise in frequency as you do.

Perhaps you have seen a demonstration of what happens when a tone with a certain frequency pattern and sufficient power is sounded in the vicinity of a crystal glass. The glass is shattered by the modulations carried in the tone. A matching pattern of sound is set up in the material that makes up the glass via resonance with the particular frequencies contained in the vibrations of the subatomic particles in the atoms and molecules that make up that material. The modulations vibrate back and forth around the core frequencies of the material and disrupt the patterns of the atomic bonds in the glass, and it shatters in response to the tone. Note that the modulation and the shattering effect is accomplished by tones that vary slightly from the prevalent tone of the material.

Each of you who is attuned to these Messages is being stimulated to emit a particular frequency pattern, and as more and more of you join in with your "notes," the collective energies and patterns will build in strength until they shatter the frequency envelope—the "glass ceiling"—that surrounds the planet. You will be shattering the energetic patterns of the existing paradigm, and opening the pathway for the emergence of a totally new world to emerge from this one. In this way, as well as the other ways we have mentioned above, you will be actively assisting in the planet's birthing into the new paradigm that will exist as Terra. All the years you have felt "out of step" with the existing paradigm are now revealed as those parts of your particular pattern that will supply the necessary deviation from the central "tone" of the existing paradigm to shatter it, on an energetic level. This is one of the reasons you have all felt so "different," as if you were "marching to a different drummer." You are! And that differentness will serve the planet by breaking the energetic bonds that maintain the material of the present paradigm.

Isn't it wonderful to know that everything you thought might be "wrong" with you is now your means to create a pathway to something utterly new? Sound and light are the elements out of which the entire Creation is formed. You bring light into the planet and you emit sound to shatter the container that has perpetuated the cycles of third-density existence. You are shattering the "glass ceiling" that has kept the planet and the people on it from advancing to the next level of being. This is a great act of service, and it has required and will continue to require much of you. The greatest act you can do to support this process is to go within, allow everything to move through you, and peacefully surrender to the process as it unfolds. By doing this, you become a "superconductor" for the higher light to enter the planet, and you emit a purer tone to shatter the glass ceiling of the existing paradigm.

There is very little you can do to affect the events that are unfolding now, except to send them love. The chief reason they occur is the lack of sufficient love on the planet. Send your love, deepen your level of acceptance, and surrender to the great force for change that is unfolding now. It is too late in the game to do much else. Join with others of like mind in whatever ways are available to you, so that you can join your sound with theirs. Give comfort and love and support to one another, also, for you have your own wounds to heal, and have need of support from others who understand. It is with great appreciation and reverence for the difficulty of your task that we leave you now, but we shall speak to you again, and soon. Amen, Adonoy Sabayoth. We are the Hosts of Heaven.

THE CROSSROADS

September 18, 2001

Dear ones, we know your hearts are heavy when you consider what is going on in the world around you. We are with you always, sheltering you with our love and showering grace upon you. We walk amongst you in human form, too, although you would not recognize us except by our actions or how you feel in our presence. But we are here, to share this journey with you, and you must know this so completely that you can feel our presence for yourself. The world will be seeing angels and devils at the same time, depending on the "glasses" being worn by the viewer. Those who harbor hate, anger, and revenge within their own heart will see devils, evil, and enemies everywhere. Those who hold the heartfelt desire for love, compassion, and a better world will see angels there to help. What one sees is a reflection of what is within. It is the way the Creator gets to see Itself, reflected in Its creations.

This notion of good and evil had served to allow people to explore duality, and it has served well. Those notions are well established in the Earth's religions and moral codes. However, it is time to put those notions aside now, as they have been exhausted in their capacity to inform you. Everything that is being put forth in the torrent of words that has flowed following the attacks [on New York City and Washington, D.C.] has been a summary of all the knowledge and beliefs that were accumulated before that time. Nothing really new is being said. No new revelations are being brought forward. Only former responses, dressed up in new clothes. The body is the same underneath, and the responses are totally predictable, based on one's views as they existed before the attacks took place.

This is a very fertile time, with many opportunities. In one sense, it is a great summing up of all the knowledge and experience that has occurred throughout all the lives that have been lived across the history of the planet. If one looks upon Earth as a laboratory, in which many experiments have taken place, this could be considered the time when the results are written up and published. Everyone can then see what has been learned from the experiments, and those conclusions provide the foundation for wholly new experiments, as life and time move on.

In each of the exchanges taking place—and there are so many now taking place—one is presented with a choice of how to respond. Will you get sucked into the chaos? Will you sit there day after day, wringing your hands and reliving the scenes over and over? Will you stop living and be glued to the television set, instead? You have a choice. You can remain caught up in the dramas, passing along the latest bit of news or "proof" of this theory or that, or you can detach and let it go. We are not saying to disregard the requests for help that come to you directly. We are not saying to not offer your prayers and love to others. We are talking about the way you feed your minds and emotions, the way you let yourself be used as a source of food for those who feed off YOUR emotions, for there are those who do that, as strange as it might seem.

It has been some time since we talked of the two polarities, and now it would be good to return to that topic. If you will recall, those of the STS [service to self] polarity are about gaining power over others. For them, there is never enough power, as the lack of love in their hearts leaves them so empty of feeling that they cannot ever have anything but the most fleeting of satisfactions. In some ways, even those who control the world's resources are among the most poverty-stricken: despite their great material wealth, they lead empty lives, built around the acquisition of things—of inanimate and abstract things that can never give or return love—and they promote death rather than life. They may have the finest wines, the finest clothing, and live the life of kings, but they are also "slaves to their habit," insatiable in their need for more and more power, more and more of everything, a lonely existence indeed. These things do not bring them happiness. These things do not bring them joy or peace. They bring them cynicism rather than hope. They bring them bitterness rather than sweetness. Their children are not free to follow their dreams. Their wives are picked because of the alliances they build, not for love. It is like the royal families in times past. They are rulers who must watch their gates, who must always be alert for those others who covet their position, who must always do things that serve their calculated ends. What pleasure is there in that? What freedom is there in that?

Therefore, the hardness of their hearts, their cynicism and contempt for the rest of the world, and the sterility of their lives leaves them empty, isolated, and bored. Business comes first, and the long walk toward the goal takes its toll, requires its own sacrifices, and leaves one more alone than before. The satisfaction of counting one's pile of money is hollow, indeed, and the simplest child who is free to play in a natural way is richer by far, in our way of measuring things.

All must play out, and if you but knew the extent to which these few have robbed the rest, you would be justifiably angry. They have robbed much more than just money and power and resources. They have robbed the world of hope, honesty, and so many of its potential joys. However, they did not get this way unaided. Every single person has contributed to their wealth and power by being part of the economic system. If you would be free of that, if you would want to stop supporting the power elite, consider what would be required. You would have to supply all of your own needs, forever. You could never make a phone call, mail a letter, turn on your oven, or take part in any of the fruits of civilization—libraries, entertainment, even your food and medicine, your homes and vehicles... Think about it. Every day, in so many countless ways, you pay for things that are the fruits of other people's labor, with money. And they labor to get money to buy the things that they need for their lives, which were in turn produced by still other people's labor.

Money is only an agreed-upon means of exchange. It has no

value in itself. And now that you have electronic communication, electronic storage of data, and the interconnection of the computers with one another across phone lines and satellites, all of your money isn't even necessary except on a local level. Everything is stored as ones and zeros in computers. Yours is a society built upon computers. Even in the most primitive regions, eventually money comes into play, and then if you trace it back to its source, there is a computer involved. So while you are angry at these people and their contempt for the rest of the world, you must also accept responsibility for giving them their power in the first place. It did not happen overnight. This move toward the centralization of power in the hands of the few has been going on for a long time—a very long time, indeed.

One of the things that will come out of the chaos in these days is an opportunity to reflect on just about everything. You will notice that, as people struggle to come to grips with what is unfolding, they run into conflicts of logic. On the one hand, some of you feel that you should not go to war, and yet you also feel that the attack cannot just be allowed to go by without a response. You are caught between two conflicting desires within yourself. You desire to be free, to not support the system that deals in wars as a solution to problems, but you also want the comforts that that system gives you. And even if you decided to go out into the wilderness somewhere and live off the land, what would that give you? Where would you go if you injured yourself? How would you survive? It is true that there are still some people on the Earth that live close to the land. Are they necessarily happy because of that, or are their lives just as filled with struggle as yours is? They spend nearly all of their time obtaining food or creating shelter or passing time through telling stories or performing rituals. They are not so different from you after all. You spend nearly all of your time "earning a living," and your stories just come in different forms—videos, movies, television programs, books, newspapers, and magazines, and personal pages on the "Web." There is not really so much difference after all.

So where are we heading with this? It is simply this: until you are able to manifest your needs directly from the matrix of Source, you will never be free. You will always be participating in a struggle for life and there will always be some who have more power than others and use it to take advantage of others for their own benefit. Are they evil? Or are they just stuck in the same prison as you? Despite their wealth, they are just as enslaved as you are. None of you has true freedom.

We have come to a place in the unfolding where you will be presented with choices of a very different nature. It will no longer be about what you will wear today, or what you will make for dinner, or when to wash the dishes. These will be fundamental choices, a kind of "final exam," with little boxes to mark on a scoring sheet. When presented with events, will you choose to descend into the pit of anger and strife or will you choose to reach higher, to transcend your mundane existence and grab hold of the next rung on the ladder toward "heaven"? We have called this Message "The Crossroads" because that represents the experience you have at this time. You will be presented with many "crossroads" in the days ahead. Which path will you choose? The one that leads downward into chaos and death or the one that leads upward into order and life? We have already described the polarities in these terms: STS is a choice for entropy, chaos, and death. STO [service to others] is a choice for order (love is the ordering force, acting on the matrix of light that underlies all form) and for life. It affirms life. These two polarities are actually two opposing forces, and their respective outcomes are predictable if you can see them clearly enough. One spiral leads downward and one spiral leads upward. You will have the opportunity, over and over again, to choose in which direction you want to go—the spiral upward or the spiral downward.

When you get caught up in ideas that there is an enemy—and there is certainly enough evidence to work with for that idea—you perpetuate the experience of being a victim. You choose the downward spiral. Are there people working in concert—a conspiracy toward certain aims? Absolutely. But are you working in concert with others to create a new world, to assist the planet in her ascension? We hope so! Is that a conspiracy, too? Are you "conspiring" to bring about "Heaven on Earth"? We hope so! There is nothing inherently evil in working together with others toward particular aims. Consider a gun. It is just a piece of metal, cast in a certain form and design. It can be used to pound in nails, as a paperweight, or as a lethal weapon. Its design is carefully crafted to be a lethal weapon, but it does not become that until someone picks it up and uses it that way.

So it is with all these ideas of "conspiracy" that are flying about at this time. If you would choose the upward spiral, you would leave those ideas behind, and not victimize yourself through them. If there are perpetrators, there are victims. Only if you wear the lenses that enable you to see the Creator wherever you look are you finally free of being a victim. Then and only then are you free of the system and from contributing toward its progress toward world domination—power over others—that is the hallmark of the STS polarity. We are saying this to you with all seriousness. This is the crossroads you will face over and over again. Will you reach upward to realize your own divinity and dwell in "heaven" or will you succumb to the chaos and choose the road to "hell"? Those are the two choices before you. There are only two. How do you choose now and how will you choose the next time the choice presents? Every time you have to choose how to respond to what is presenting will be another crossroads for you. You will find it easier over time, because you will have left the other choices behind, and as you discover that you prefer to continue in the direction in which you find peace.

We leave you now in peace and honor and blessing. Amen, Adonoy Sabayoth. We are the Hosts of Heaven.

MANY WORLDS, MANY DESTINATIONS
September 27, 2001

All right, now. We have asked to speak to you today to broaden your understanding of what is unfolding on your perceptual screen. There is a complexity involved that is quite frankly beyond that which your conscious mind can grasp. And so we ask that, as you read these words, that you also open yourself to receive a deeper knowing, a deeper trust of the process that has begun and will continue until it is totally complete.

To retrace our steps a bit, we would return to the idea we gave you about the Mind of the Creator, as a matrix that contains all things that have been and will be. Each thing or event that emerges from that matrix contains within itself all of the elements for its completion—all the events that will play out within the container or envelope of that event are anticipated and come forth from the Creator Itself. Each event can be viewed as a "thought" of the Creator, thinking to Itself and exploring all of the possibilities that are available to It. These possibilities are essentially infinite, and it is easy to get lost in trying to contemplate the infinitely branching tree that makes up the Mind of the Creator, what we will call the Tree of Mind. In the Tree of Mind, every possible branch is explored through the mechanism of parallel realities. Each time there is a decision point reached, a branch is created to accommodate all possible decisions that can be experienced within that situation. Within a given Creation, there are some parameters that govern that particular Creation, and the possibilities that are available within that Creation are limited to the constraints of those parameters, which we have called Universal Laws. This much we have said before.

So, how does this relate to what you are experiencing? It works something like this: In your present experience of the Creation, there are many event envelopes overlapping each other and seeming to occupy the same space. As you look around you with your physical senses, you think that you are seeing the same thing as everyone else does, and in fact to some extent you do. But there is another mechanism operating also, which we have referred to before—the splitting off or separating out of all of the parallel "futures" that will emerge from your one shared reality—the planet you call Earth. All of these different event envelopes are heading in different directions and those of you who are in the "Terra" envelope are heading in that direction, while those who are in other envelopes are heading in other directions. Where it gets complex is when one tries to grasp how it all fits together—or even how it all comes apart!

We cannot even begin to address the complexity involved, it is so vast, so we will confine ourselves to discussing the path to Terra and one other world—Terra's mirror world, the destination that is equal to Terra, but of the opposite polarity. There are many other paths that are also occurring, but far too many for us to explore, and they do not illuminate your path as well as the contrast afforded by this one other, which shall remain unnamed.

You will recall that we have said that the polarization on the planet will increase as things move forward in time, and you see that happening now. It will continue to proceed toward even more polarization, so things will intensify along all of the paths being traversed, but these two paths—to Terra and to its polar opposite—will experience this polarization at its most extreme. All of the other paths lead to other worlds, for further exploration of other themes and experiences. These two worlds are the only ones that will be purely 4D in their vibration and expression, and since Terra is one of these two worlds, the timeline that leads to Terra contains the mirrored expression of the other world, at least for a time. By the time you are lifted off of the planet, those two paths will have split off from one another, but while you are still involved in the lifting—even if you leave and come back—you will be witnessing the mirror provided by this other world and path. And we should also mention that many people will not be going to Terra, but to their own "home systems," for a period of rest, recovery and exploration that does not involve either of these two worlds at all. And some of THOSE worlds are "higher" in frequency than Terra, so it really is a very complex process, indeed!

All this being said, as the Earth ascends toward her destiny of becoming Terra, those who are on these two timelines—the one to Terra and the one to her opposite—will be in each other's view for awhile. Being that you are the "caring kind" of people, it could be difficult for you to witness the playing out of the most extreme forms of the negative-polarity behaviors by those who are seeking to graduate to that other world. If you can see their actions as that— that they are having their "final exams" also—you might be able to comprehend the force that drives them to their goal—the world of THEIR dreams—just as you can comprehend your own passion to achieve your goal of Terra—the world of YOUR dreams. To you, their dreams are a waking nightmare, but you actually have much more in common than you might think. You both seek a global form of government, a common set of values, and a way to live within the available resources. However, the MEANS of achieving those goals is where you differ. You emphasize the empowerment of everyone, and they emphasize their own empowerment at the expense of everyone else. STO and STS, pure and simple.

This is the Creator's dream, and the Creator wants to experience everything, from every possible perspective. The Creator wants to experience all of the possibilities and gets to experience them through Its creations and their interaction with each other. The Creator does not JUDGE Its creations as "good" and "bad." The Creator expresses through Its creations, and having created them, considers them ALL "good." They all exist to satisfy the Creator's desire to know Itself through Its infinite possible manifestations. When it says in the Bible that God looked at Its creation and was pleased, this is how the Creator views Its creations. It is "pleased" by ALL of its creations, not just the ones you would prefer to experience. You are the Creator-in-expression, seeking a particular pole of expression. There are others who are seeking the opposite pole, and from the Creator's perspective, they are just as "good" as you are. You are repelled by those things that are not like you. That helps to define your experience and propel you in the direction of your seeking. It is just as true of these others of the opposite pole. They have contempt for and are repelled by those who are not like THEM and that helps propel THEM in the direction of THEIR seeking. At the core of it, it is ALL just the Creator, playing with Itself through all the possibilities made available by all Its creations.

So, from the Creator's point of view, both Terra and its opposite—this all-negative-polarity world—are equally good, because they provide the Creator with the opportunity to fully explore those two opposite poles. All of the OTHER worlds that emerge from this one shared reality that you call "Earth" will be spread across the spectrum BETWEEN those two poles and have varying proportions of that mixture of STO and STS. There will be worlds that are primarily inclining toward STO, and as they progress, some of those people will incarnate on Terra as babies born to those who are already there. There will be worlds that will be primarily STS and they will progress to the world that is Terra's opposite and incarnate there. And there will be still other worlds that remain somewhat mixed and be rich environments in which to explore both poles, and they will progress in that way for many thousands of years until another grand cycle is completed and another opportunity presents for a harvest to one pole or the other. The unfolding of the Creator's dream is endless, and the paths of possibilities branch and branch and branch again, over and over and over, throughout eternity. There is no end to the dream.

So, in your experience now, you will be seeing an intensification of the two polarities of behaviors. The "in-between" will fade from your view. You can best see and understand yourself and your path in two ways: by reflecting off of its mirror opposite and by finding others like yourself with whom you can share your own views, your own feelings, your own experiences. We have said that if you engage with "us and them" thinking, you risk being caught up in the morass, the downward spiral into darkness and more confusion. It is all right to witness the opposite pole, as it helps you to understand what you are NOT, but it is imperative that you detach from IDENTIFYING with it. It helps to remind you of who you are, but it does not DEFINE who you are. To the extent that you can tune out the horrors that are coming, you will preserve yourself and your self-identity. This does not mean that you should close your heart. Just the opposite! What we are saying is that you must disconnect from feeling RESPONSIBLE for what is appearing on your perceptual screen.

What is appearing on your perceptual screen is sourcing from the Creator. Each person is simply being who they came to be, according to the plan for their life. Each person is perfectly situated to make their contribution to the rich mix of experiences playing out now, and there are no "bad" creations. Each "evil" is part of the "good." Each player is needed for the entire experience to be complete. Each event envelope contains all the elements for its completion and the entire "set" of elements is interwoven and interacting in ways that you simply cannot grasp with your mind. But your SOUL and your HEART can FEEL the truth of this, and this understanding can allow you to unlock your own potential for love. You will do best to cultivate compassion when you encounter suffering, to let yourself be deepened and hollowed out by your compassion, to keep your hearts open and tender and vulnerable and at the same time be deepened until all that you are is love.

You are not responsible for what you are seeing. You did not create it. You do not have to beat yourself about the head and shoulders in penance for some sin you committed. Everything you are, everything you have done, is all within the plan for your life. The place you CAN be responsible is for your own RESPONSES to the situation. Your own responses are your own process of working out who you are, why you are here, and where you are going. You are one aspect of the Creator, providing the Creator with a particular experience through the locus of your perception as an individualized aspect of the Creator. If you must "blame" anyone, you must blame the Creator. If you must be angry, you must be angry at the Creator. Everywhere you look, everything you see, is the Creator-in-expression. The people who die are the Creator. The people who kill them are the Creator. If you can just "get" this, you will have peace, you will transcend the phenomenal reality, and you will be that much closer to "home."

We leave you now, in peace and honor and blessing. Amen, Adonoy Sabayoth. We are the Hosts of Heaven.

"STEADY AS SHE GOES"
October 2, 2001

All right, then. We have asked to speak to you today because there are numerous shocks on the horizon, and we wanted to give you a possible way of being with them that will greatly facilitate your comfort as you move towards your goal.

If you think about your oceans, you will have an ideal model for what we are talking about. On the surface of these great bodies of water, there is great variation in the activity one sees—from placid calm to rolling waves to great turbulence and violent storms. So it is with your world of everyday living. It varies tremendously, from placid calm and moments of true peace through varying degrees of instability, stress, and outright crisis. If one goes deeply down into the depths of the oceans, there are powerful currents and a rich absence of turbulence—a profound presence of silence, power, and potential adventure, encased in a soothing smoothness of texture and sound. If you withdraw from your ordinary world and dive deeply within, it is similar. There you will find a profound presence of power, potential adventure, and a deep, calming release.

So as these storms come into the world about you, it would be wise to take refuge in the deep stillness within yourself, to experience the safety of that, to follow the deep currents of your life, and to thread your way through the vast oceans of inner space toward your goal.

In wartime, there is a ship called a submarine. It makes use of reflected sound, much as the dolphins and whales find their way in their watery home. A sound is sent out and then returned, so the distance from other objects is sensed and they can be avoided. You send out your sound into the universe and it is returned to you, guiding you through the waters ahead as you slide forward, toward your goal.

The submarine can dive deep, to avoid detection at the surface, and to get to its goal and deliver its payload or cargo. In wartime, there are minefields that must be traversed. There are sometimes explosions nearby. It takes a skilled hand and steady nerves to traverse the oceans and move steadily toward one's goal. When the captain of a submarine is satisfied with the vessel's direction, depth, and speed, he calls to the crew, "Steady as she goes." By this, he communicates that the ship should maintain its direction, depth, and speed, until and unless he gives a different command. We would say that our "sub" toward Terra has begun its voyage through the oceans of inner space. We left the old world behind on August 18 and have been increasing our depth and speed ever since. In a few short days, we will begin traversing the mine fields and there will be explosions all around, but our direction will always be "Steady as she goes." So it is with you. In your voyage through these times, you must say to yourself, "Steady as she goes." You must stay steady on your course to Terra, let the explosions happen as they will, and have the sure knowledge that whatever happens around you, you will not waver at the helm.

Steady as she goes. Remain steady and stay the course. Keep your eyes on the goal. Steady as she goes. Let the rest fall around you. Steady as she goes. Your path is straight, you are protected. Steady as she goes... Steady as she goes... Steady as she goes.

Feel the quiet. Listen to your breathing as it comes in softly and goes out again. Listen to the distant sounds of war and know you are safe. Steady as she goes. Feel the dull impacts of the explosions. Steady as she goes. Check your fuel supply. You are fine. Steady as she goes... Steady as she goes... Steady as she goes.

As these days unfurl in front of you, remind yourself, "Steady as she goes." You can do this. You came to do this. This is why you are here. Hold your course. Hold your speed. Stay below the surface events and "Steady as she goes." Steady as she goes. Distant sounds, distant storms, but steady as she goes.

Each of you has come for this, for this time, for this task. Steady as she goes... Steady as she goes. Hold the vision; seek the goal. Steady as she goes... Steady as she goes... Steady as she goes.

Take this Message and read it again. Steady as she goes. Keep it with you to remind you. Steady as she goes... Steady as she goes.

Time is passing now and each day takes you closer to the goal. Steady as she goes... Steady as she goes.

Remind yourself how far you have come. Not much further to go. Steady as she goes... Steady as she goes. Be steady in your course and speed. Steady as she goes.

We are with you now, guiding you, protecting you, sheltering you. Dive deep. Stay deep. Follow your course. Steady as she goes... Steady as she goes. Make a shelter for yourself, create the stillness where you are. Turn off the madness, the screaming, the crying, the pleading. Steady as she goes... Steady as she goes. Turn off the madness. Steady as she goes... Steady as she goes... Steady as she goes.

Hear the water sliding by. Steady as she goes. Hear the muffled roar and thunderous crashing of storms and wind-driven waves overhead. Go deep. Stay deep. Steady as she goes... Steady as she goes.

We are with you, every day, every night—guiding you, loving you, protecting you. Steady as she goes. Leave behind the surface world. Seek the power of deep ocean. Follow your course. Leave behind the madness. Steady as she goes.

In time... with sufficient time... you will emerge in your new reality, but for now, you must glide through the deep waters of deep ocean. Steady as she goes. Keep your eyes on the goal. Steady as she goes.

We leave you now in peace and honor and blessing, but we are with you in your dreams, in your waking, in your sailing through the deep waters. Steady as she goes... Steady as she goes. Amen, Adonoy Sabayoth. We are the Hosts of Heaven. Steady as she goes.

"Take a look at the world around you, as it is right now, for it will soon pass away altogether. Take a look at it as if you were suddenly told that you had but a few years to live, for in fact, that is the truth. You have only a few years left before this entire stage will be swept bare and none of what you can see will remain."

(AUTHOR'S NOTE: The following excerpts from the Old Testament prophesy the Pole Shift. This description comes very close to what I saw in my 1982 vision (page 140), but I was not aware of this passage until I saw it referred to in a book I was reading when this second edition was being prepared for the printer.)

ISAIAH, CHAPTER 24

BEHOLD, the LORD shall destroy the earth and lay it waste and turn it upside down and scatter its inhabitants.

3 The land shall be utterly destroyed and utterly spoiled; for the LORD has spoken this word.

13 For thus it shall be in the midst of the land among the peoples, it shall be as the shaking of an olive tree and as the gleaning of grapes when the vintage is done.

19 The earth is utterly broken down, the earth is utterly moved, the earth is staggering exceedingly.

20 The earth shall reel to and fro like a drunkard and shall be shaken like a booth ...and it shall fall and not rise again.

23 Then the moon shall be [blocked] and the sun [hidden], for the LORD of hosts ...will be glorified in the presence of his saints.

(from the George M. Lamsa translation; see "Suggested Reading" on page 156.)

A LAST LOOK AROUND

October 9, 2001

All right, now. Everything we said was coming has now arrived at your door, but there is so much more to the picture than you see at this moment in time. There are things arriving into your reality that are beyond your wildest imagination—of both kinds. Side by side, now, you will witness—literally—the "greatest show on Earth." You will see things occur of unspeakable majesty and beauty and you will see things of unspeakable horror and tragedy. Both will occur side by side.

The human species has the capability for both of these extremes—ecstasy and agony. It has the ability to create them and to experience them. And indeed, throughout the human journey on Earth, it has done both, over and over again. But now, as the final years dwindle away, it is time for the grand finale—the last "act" of the human drama on this planet, at this density, for a very, very long time.

And so we would ask you to take a last look around before it is gone. Take a look at the world around you, as it is right now, for it will soon pass away altogether. Take a look at it as if you were suddenly told that you had but a few years to live, for in fact, that is the truth. You have only a few years left before this entire stage will be swept bare and none of what you can see will remain. But even before THAT, the world as you have known it—as you have taken it for granted would always be there—will be radically changed. The

71

wars that are beginning now are just the beginning of the changes. Everything in the human experience will be revisited in some way, if not at a global level, then at a personal and individual level. All of your "personal histories," across all of the lives that were created throughout time, will be summed up now, and you will find that any remnants of old patterns will come flying back in your face to be balanced and cleared so that you can finally move beyond them—beyond this world and all of its experiences, altogether.

So how would you feel if you were told you had, say, 18 months to live? What would your priorities be? How important would it be to plan a "next career," or to plan anything, for that matter? What would you want to do most if you had only 18 months left? Who would you talk to? What would you say? Where would you want to live? What would you want to do? Is there some unfinished business left in your life? What do you need to do now to finish it? We suggest that you begin to think in these ways now, as there is not much more time than that left for you to do those sorts of things. That is not to say that there will be a Pole Shift in 18 months, but we are saying that the world will be so different by then that the time will be over for these kinds of questions for you.

We are not saying that there is an urgency or emergency about this. What we are saying is that you should treasure these last days of relative normalcy as they are fast disappearing and will never be seen again. Despite the wars that are beginning, it will be a while before they extend to the entire world. It will be a while before the food supplies are gone for much of the world's populations. It will be a while before the technology is in place that will create a global surveillance system. It will be a while, but it will not be much longer.

So take a last look around you. Savor all that it is to be a human being. Spend some time reflecting on your memories before you pack them away forever. Take some extra time with your loved ones, and consider what is really important to you now. Savor the seasons and their moods. Savor the good things of life, without being extravagant. Find balance. Be good to yourself in ways that are truly nourishing—good food, good friends, and "quality time" with those you care about. Say "no" to the pressures that keep you on the treadmill of doing and start spending more time being. The things that fill you are the simple ones—a hand held, a sunset, the passage of a flight of birds through the sky. Feel your connection to the planet. Feel your connection to the stars. Feel your connection to the entire span of the human drama, in all of its forms, in all of its ages, and in all of its color and richness and moods.

Look at the animals around you and give them more love, too. Give your trees a hug. Give your plants a special treat—perhaps some fresh soil or a new pot. Show your appreciation for all of life and it will appreciate you in return.

How often do you take time to appreciate yourself? In your habits, in your conditioning, there is so much criticism to offer—of others, of yourself, of the way the world is run. How much time do you take to appreciate your world? Do it now. Do it more often. Make it a new habit.

When you sit down to a meal, do you take a moment to appreciate it? Or is it something that is taken for granted? There are many in the world who will not have a meal tonight, or the next night, or the night after that. Appreciate your meal. Appreciate the life that was given by the plants and the animals so that you could have that meal. Appreciate the work that was done by the growers, the pickers, and the preparers so that you could have that meal. If you have good health, appreciate that. If you have pain, appreciate that. Appreciate your ability to feel, to see, to hear, to draw breath. There are many who cannot do even that.

Celebrate life in a quiet way. Soften your walk, soften your talk. Be good to yourself and to others. If you buy something, appreciate it enough to make it a worthwhile purchase. Instead of "making do," make it special. That does not mean it has to be costly. It means you have to take the time and attention to ask yourself what it is you would really enjoy. Live your life with conscious attention. Consider the invisible web that binds you to others through everything you do in every day. When you turn on the water at the sink, someone else made that possible for you to do. When you lie down in your bed at night, someone else made that possible for you to do. Someone made the bed. Someone made the sheets. Someone delivered it to the store where it was bought. Someone built the room in which you lie. Maybe it was you, but then you used materials that someone else made available.

Take a last look around and see how everything there is was made possible in so many ways by so many people around the world. There already is a global economy and no part exists in isolation from the others. You already are part of a global society, and what happens in one part of the world affects every other part. There is no movement made, no breath drawn, anywhere in the world that does not affect every other part in the world, whether you are aware of it or not. Appreciate your connection to everything else. It is there. You can feel it. FEEL it! Don't think about it so much. Feel it. Feel how you are part of the intricate web of life, of the flow of life and even of death. Appreciate these days and appreciate all that you are in these days, for you are changing, too.

We have talked about a homecoming, but there is also a home-leaving. You are all going to be going to somewhere else very soon, so appreciate your life and your world now as if you are seeing it for the first time, so you will be complete with it when it is time to go. You are going to be off on a grand adventure, one that will take you beyond all things that you know now, but to complete with THIS world with grace and ease, take time to take that last look around, knowing that you will be leaving soon.

When we say "soon," that is relative, but even within the span of your present time, it will be soon enough. Soon enough for you to leave while you can still remember this world as it is now. Long enough for you to be glad to move on to another world with no backward glances or things undone. It is time, now, to face these things. It is time, now, to do these things. It is time, now.

We have said before to allow all things. We say now to embrace all things. We have said before to let go of your attachments, to receive the lifting. We say now to hold out your hand, your heart, and your soul to receive the richness of your life now. Be grateful for all things, large and small. Be in an "attitude of gratitude" and you will feel yourself blessed beyond counting. In the midst of the wars, you can have peace, you can have joy, and you can share love. The wars will go on 'till it's over, but you can live fully and joyfully in their midst. We do not say this lightly. You hold the template of a new tomorrow and as the dying proceeds, so does the birthing. Just as in life things pass away in their time, so too, does new life come and bring the promise of a new day. Yesterday and tomorrow meet in the ever-present NOW. Yesterday and tomorrow are defined by the present moment, the bead on the string that moves steadily toward its destiny. You are the dawn-bringers and after the twilight fades and the world is engulfed in darkness, you will come again with the light, to wipe away the tears and bring peace.

Amen, Adonoy Sabayoth. We are the Hosts of Heaven. We leave you now in peace and honor and blessing and shall speak with you again.

"In your historical past, there have been isolated individuals who have walked this path and there have been some isolated groups of people who have also made this journey, but this has never before happened on a global scale, and most certainly not for the planet itself."

ASCENSION IS A PROCESS, PART ONE
October 17, 2001

All right, now. We have asked to speak to you today to give you our perspective on the process of ascension, as it is being experienced in your space/time reality. We have qualified our remarks by that last phrase—as it is being experienced in your space/time reality. The process you are undergoing and experiencing now is different in several ways from what has been described in the "literature" that has reached you regarding this process/event. This process has never before occurred on your planet on a mass scale, and not only is a portion of the human species ascending now, but the planet and everything on her is being subjected to the same process of rising through the vibrational layers. In your historical past, there have been isolated individuals who have walked this path and there have been some isolated groups of people who have also made this journey, but this has never before happened on a global scale, and most certainly not for the planet itself.

Therefore, the descriptions of this process that have reached you have been vague and lacking in detail. The most explicit writings that have survived have described an apparent "event," as if ascension took place in an instant. In some rare cases, the process did indeed appear to come to a head rather suddenly, as if a threshold was crossed and things changed rather markedly, but even if this is what happened then, this is NOT what is happening now. For you who are bound for Terra, your ascension is ongoing and will be a process that continues long after the Earth itself has ascended to her glorified form, as Terra. We want to go into some detail today about how that is occurring and what to expect as the process proceeds.

Let us begin with some basics, to summarize some of the ground we have already covered in our prior communications with you. The process of ascension involves a change in frequency of vibration and a change in consciousness that carries with it some other phenomena and abilities. You are engaged in this process now, and you are already experiencing some of the changes in perception that go with this change. That will continue and grow more evident as things progress through linear time. It has ALREADY happened, when viewed from outside of time, but since your focus of attention is presently located from within the experience of linear time, we are describing things from your present view, rather than ours.

Most, if not all, of you reading this have been experiencing many of the symptoms of this process. We have mentioned before the bodily changes that are involved, and the clearings that take place as each successive frequency band is traversed. You are by now quite familiar with some of this, and as things proceed, those things will continue, as well. Your preferences in foods, in music—in every aspect of your life—will shift with the ongoing change in your consciousness. Your energy levels will fluctuate greatly as you withdraw from those things that used to fascinate you and begin to move more inward. You will find your need for rest increasing, as your energy becomes more involved with integrating the ongoing cellular activity and your bodies prepare for your new forms to occur. You may become more sensitive to stresses in the Earth's crust, to disturbances in the electromagnetic spectrum, and to some of the technologies being employed by the power elite. You can support your transition in many ways, but the key word here is self-nourishment. Do those things that make YOU more comfortable. Because you are of the STO-polarity orientation, it is natural for you to want to turn your energies outward toward serving others, but it is at this time that you need to prepare yourself for your subsequent service, which requires that you take care of your own needs first at this time. If you take the longer view, all of the care that you give to yourself and those close to you now will be an "investment" in the treasure that you will make available to others when the time comes for you to do that.

Think of it this way: You have a tool you call a ratchet. It is used to turn things like screws and bolts in a forward direction and makes use of the leverage of torque. After each turn forward, the ratchet pulls back and powers up for the next turn forward. The screws and the bolts are constructed with spiral tracks on them that cause them to move forward by being turned or cycled by the tool that turns them. The ratchet provides forward motion by dropping back to power up for the next thrust forward. The spiral is the shape of evolution, and each turn on the spiral is a movement forward as well as outward or inward. By withdrawing and turning your energies toward your own process and comfort now, you are powering up your next turn on the spiral, your next movement forward and outward, and you are becoming the agent for service beyond that which you are capable of now. So look at this time of withdrawal as being the ratchet, gathering energy for the next movement forward and outward. You will be in center stage soon enough, but this is your process now, in preparation for that next movement in your lives.

So this process of ascension involves a withdrawal from the world around you. Many, if not most, of you are feeling this now, and some of you are not knowing how to be with that experience. We have talked much about the necessity of withdrawing and detaching from the drama around you. We want to emphasize how necessary this is to your process now. The world around you will get along without your need to feed it with your energy now. It is on a crash course with oblivion and will pass away within the next few years. You are not needed in this world now. Your task now is to prepare for your service at the end of this world and to blaze the pathway to the next reality that will follow. There is nothing for you to do with regard to stopping what is playing out in the amphitheater, the drama you see on the world's perceptual screen. You are playing in a different play now, and that dying world is supposed to die. All of the symptoms of past human experience are leaving the planet, are coming up to view as they exit this plane. It is all being flushed to the surface in a grand cleansing of all that has gone before and it is a purification for the planet and everything on her. It is not helped by resistance on your part. It is helped by your allowing the process to unfold, to accept the process for what it is, and for you to stop giving it your energy and attention. All attempts to stop what is going on are forms of resistance and only make things more intense. Every particle of resistance requires a matching energy to overcome it, so if you can "let go and let God" take care of the process, you will be doing the highest and best thing you can for the smoothest transition for all.

Ascension is a process, not an event. There is a threshold that is crossed at some point in the process when the veil has fallen away and one can see fully. But that is only one minute step in a long journey. Ascension does not end when the veil falls. The journey continues forever, with the inbreath back into the Godhead, the dissolving away of separate identity, and the emergence again as a separate identity with the next outbreath from the Godhead. It is all just the Creator, breathing Itself out into expression, inhaling Itself back into Itself, and breathing Itself out into expression again. This process never ends and the journey of experience never ends, so it will be helpful to your process if you can accept that there is no "ending" in sight for you. You will go on, eternally, also, for you are the expression of the Creator and that never ends—for you or for the Creator.

So those of you who might be expecting an "event" need to readjust your thinking a bit. Think of a movie you have seen. Each frame of the movie exists as a separate "event," but they all blend together seamlessly in an event flow that is experienced more like a process than as separate events. Each breath you take is an "event," but you take for granted the process that occurs when you breathe. The air enters you, the oxygen moves into your bloodstream and enters your cells, and from there, each atom of oxygen participates in different chemical processes. Then those atoms combine with other atoms and new compounds are made, energy is produced, and end products such as carbon dioxide are passed out into the bloodstream to be carried to your lungs and exhaled. Think of it! All of this is going on in your body with every breath you take! All of this is going on in your body with every breath you exhale. Every breath is an event, but each breath—each event—is part of a larger process, in which your body functions, you experience life through all of your senses, and the whole complexity of life as you know it proceeds.

So it is with this ascension process. It is made up of many "events," strung together in a process that is complex and experienced through all of your senses. There are cycles in this process and there is a movement forward and upward, followed by a time of integration. This integration process requires energy. It requires energy that would normally be given to other activities. When you fix your attention on the drama, you are taking away energy from your ascension and giving it to the drama. You are not supporting your ascension as fully as you might, so we would ask you to give your ascension the priority over the drama, if you are not already doing so. If you are heading toward Terra, your life will be more difficult for you if you do not align fully with your ascension. Your resistance will require that life provides a force in your life that is sufficient to overcome your resistance, so that you can fulfill your life's goal.

Your life has a plan to it—a built-in direction in which you must go—and your thoughts and impulses arise from the Oversoul that creates you as an expression of itself. Your Oversoul has made you the way you are, down to the color of your eyelashes and your preference for a certain type of food. However, you are not an island, floating in the emptiness of space. You live in a rich matrix of experience, and being sensitive, you can easily get caught up in the swirl of emotions that are flooding your experiential field from so many sources. Your media play on those emotions as a way of getting you to do things, such as buy certain products or engage in certain behaviors. Your political machine plays on those emotions to further that agenda. Your power elite play on those emotions to get you to go in the direction they want you to go. If you want to be free, if you want to be sovereign, you need to detach from the drama. You need to find ways of being "in the world," but not "of it." If you work for a living, you need to find a way of continuing to do that without getting caught up in the emotions that are swirling around you. You don't have to tune them out altogether. That would probably be impossible to maintain, anyway. What you have to learn to do is become TRANSPARENT to them—to let them pass without engaging with them in a similar fashion. If someone around you is upset, you don't have to join them in being upset. If someone near you is angry, you don't have to engage with them from that kind of energy. You can be calm in the midst of the chaos, and it will be much better for you if you do so.

The process of ascension is already underway. It is unstoppable at this point and the cleansing is unstoppable also. Your only meaningful response is to step back and create an island of calm in yourself. Create that space within you, and if you find yourself getting caught up in the drama, bring yourself gently back to that space of calm as soon as you become aware that you have left it. That is why meditation is such good training for this process. In meditation, inevitably your mind wanders and thoughts come. It is a discipline to bring your mind gently back to the breath or whatever it is you are focusing on in your meditation. It is a discipline to bring yourself back to your center and calm whenever you find yourself getting caught up in the drama. By cultivating this habit of remaining calm and centered in the midst of the chaos, you will be a great force—collectively speaking—for calm in the midst of chaos in the world.

You hold a template within yourself, and these Messages are an attunement device that is energizing that template through more and more people all over the world. You are widely separated from each other because you must cover the globe and there are so few of you to do this task now. As each person finds their way to this material and comes into resonance with it, a field effect is created that is so powerful, you would have trouble comprehending it. You are like a growing wave, enveloping the planet—bringing in the higher light and grounding it into the planet; radiating out the new pattern of energy and shattering the existing paradigm by your holding forth this way of being in the midst of the chaos.

You are peaceful warriors—warriors for truth, warriors for peace and love and joy. Your "mission" is to simply BE where you are, holding forth what you are, holding the vision and promise of Terra, holding your place in the world, letting things unfold and holding steady in the midst of it all. The interesting thing about this is that when you do this, you create that reality that you want to live in, right where you are. You CREATE a little bit of Terra, right now, where you are. You CREATE peace by being at peace. You CREATE love by resting in love. You CREATE joy by allowing your joy to exist in the midst of so much sorrow. Life has beauty that you can perceive. Focus on beauty, and you will become beautiful. Your inner radiance will bless all who come in contact with you, and you will birth beauty in the midst of the horror.

All your life, you felt out of step with the rest of the world. Well, you are STILL out of step with the rest of the world and now you know why. The rest of the world is passing away and you are the bringers of the new dawn on the horizon. You are stepping forth in your role as co-creators of a new reality, and your path runs counter to that of the rest of the world. You have been out of step because you are paving a new road, a road that leads to freedom. You are not going in the same direction as the rest of the world, and so you are diverging more and more each day from the direction they are taking. You must do exactly what others are not willing or able to do. You must be what you came to be and do what you came to do. It is a solitary thing for you for now, but a day is coming when you will be rejoined with the others and there is a gathering taking place even now. You are being gathered onto your road, that road that goes to Terra, and you are leaving behind the other roads that lead to other destinations.

Follow your calling. Follow that inner voice that leads you, step by step, in the direction of your destiny. Step out onto that untraveled road that unfurls before you now. You are creating it with every step you take and we are with you, supporting each and every step, so it is a collective undertaking. We are a team—those of us in the higher realms, and those of you who are walking this road on the ground. We shall speak more on this subject, but for now we leave you in peace and honor and blessing. We love you and are with you at all times, and you are well on your way home. It is not much further now. You can do this. It is what you came to do.

Amen, Adonoy Sabayoth. We are the Hosts of Heaven.

ASCENSION IS A PROCESS, PART TWO
November 9, 2001

All right, now. We have said we would continue our conversation about the ascension process, and it is time for us to do that now.

First of all, we wish to reiterate that the lifting we have spoken of is a process that will culminate in an "event"—the crossing of a threshold into the next frequency band. This lifting has two components to it: a physical component, related to the spin frequency of the subatomic particles in your physical body, and a spiritual component, related to a shift in your consciousness and ways of perceiving your reality. Both are taking place at the same time and interrelate, as consciousness affects all physical materiality.

There is no way to separate consciousness from the physical manifestation of matter. Consciousness is the ground, or matrix, out of which physical matter emerges. We have spoken of the Mind of the Creator as the matrix for all of the Creation, and your individualized consciousness is a portion of that Infinite Mind, as long as you are still veiled and in the experience of separation. Once your veils have fallen and the barrier is removed, you will be in full and continuous communion with the Mind of the Creator and when you have learned to operate from that platform, you will be able to affect, alter, and create material reality from that place of infinite blessing. All of the powers of the Creator will be vested in your individual locus of attention, and you will consciously be aware of yourselves as the creator-gods you have always been.

Those of you who are bound for Terra are the first genera-tion—the product of the first Thought—of the Creator. You are the Elohim, and though you do not remember this fully now, you will once your shift is complete. Over the next 18 months, you will find yourself much changed. The dropping away of your old life will continue, at an accelerated pace. Your fascination with the things of 3D will wane even more than before, and you will gradually detach from identifying with the 3D reality as your reality. You will begin to access more and more of your 4D identity and personality, and you will begin to access more and more of the 4D way of doing things. You must trust this process and trust your "knowing" that you are safe, sane, and that all is proceeding according to plan.

Some of you are being asked by the circumstances of your life to move on—either to other places of residence or to other people, leaving behind those aspects of your old life. This is part of the sorting out into the different destinations, and we would counsel you to be at peace in the midst of this change. If fear arises, open the breath. Close your eyes for a moment and focus on deepening and opening your breath. Relax into the breath and feel your body relax into the truth of the moment. You are safe. Your world is changing, but you are safe. The world around you may be tumbling down, but you are safe. Remind yourself of this whenever things seem to be moving beyond your ability to control them. You don't need to control anything anymore. We are carrying you on a swift river of change, and we are with you at all times. You are surrounded by more help and protection than you could ever know. If you need to feel our presence, quiet yourself and go within. When you have become quiet and calm, you can invite us to reveal ourselves to you and you will be able to feel us in your own unique way. We are with you, but if you cannot quiet yourself, you will not be able to feel our presence and take comfort in that. As within, so without. When you are peaceful inside, you will draw peaceful energies to you from the outside.

Peace, peace, peace. It is so important to find and create inner peace. As the world around you moves steadily into more strife and war, create peace within and detach from the drama. Be like the Buddha. Be like the Christ. Be like all of those world teachers who have come to show the way—who knew the eternal truths of existence. You will be like them when this process is complete. You will be like them when it is time for you to return for those who are going to need your help and comfort, who will need you to lead them to safety before the Pole Shift occurs.

This is a process, but there is also an "event" aspect to it. When it is the perfect time, the missing ingredient will be supplied and a door will open into another plane of reality. This is not something you can do for yourself at this time. It will be offered to you at the perfect time and in the perfect way for your particular circumstances. All of those who are meant to go with you will go with you at that time. They will be with you and you will cross through the door together—your children, your animals, your friends and family members who have chosen for Terra will go with you. You may have children, friends, and family members who have NOT chosen to go to Terra and they will not go with you. All will happen in the perfect way for your particular circumstances. This is being done in love and we ask you to remember that love is the opposite of fear. If you are in fear about this, you will not be able to receive it. Let go and let God. It is still the answer to all questions. Let go and let God handle the details. We know what we are doing, and it will all be done perfectly for each individual situation.

Your task in all of this is to prepare yourselves to receive the changes with as much grace and ease as you can. Surrender is the way through. Resistance will only increase your discomfort. Let go and let God. If you look at those around you, love them enough to trust that they will have exactly the right experience for their life plan. If their Oversoul has chosen for them to go to Terra, they will, regardless of what they know or don't know, regardless of what they believe or don't believe. These Messages are beginning to affect enough people that a change in the field of the mass consciousness is beginning to be noticed by those who are receptive to it. You are resonating it into being. In the midst of all that is going on in the world, you are affecting things through your combined energies. Your longing for Terra is creating an energetic pathway toward it that will open it up for more and more people as things proceed.

This is your work in this world at this moment—to create that energetic pathway toward Terra. You are like the icebreaker ships that clear a passage for others to follow. It may not seem like you are doing anything, but if you will pay attention to your own transformation—how you yourselves are changing—you will recognize that you are radiating out a different "signal" than those around you who are still blindly following the ways of 3D.

You are all embodying the higher light. You are experiencing some discomforts as those attachments and those conditions that are not in keeping with your essence are purged from your cellular memory and from your life circumstances. This is a good time to simplify your lives. By that, we do not mean you have to become ascetics. We are merely suggesting that "less is more." If you still have clutter in your life, get rid of the clutter. If you have possessions that no longer reflect your present tastes or interests, get rid of them. Open up space in your homes, your lives. Say goodbye to those things that no longer serve you, with thanks for what they have been for you and to you. They have served, but when they no longer serve you, get rid of them. The less you have left of the things that remind you of what you were, the easier it will be to receive what you are becoming. You can still keep photographs if they still have energy for you. You can still keep books if they still have energy for you. But those things that don't have energy for you anymore—get rid of them. Be discerning, and by doing these things, you will make yourself more aware of how you have changed.

You will continue to change, and your tastes and interests will continue to change. One day you may be drawn to something and soon afterward you will be through with it. No blame. Just accept the process and move smoothly through it, touching on those things that present in your life to be touched upon. If there is one quality that will characterize this process, it is impermanence. Nothing will remain the same. You are changing daily, so it makes sense that your relationship to your world will also be changing daily. As things proceed, you will become skilled at surfing the wave of change. You will become more accustomed to maintaining your balance and staying over your feet as the wave of change carries you toward your destination—Terra. In surfing, the key to a successful ride on the wave is staying right over your feet. If you lean back too far or forward too far, you will tumble into the wave. If you remain anywhere but over your feet, you lose your balance and the ride is over for the moment, requiring you to get back up and regain your balance again.

We have spoken a little about how it is on Terra—how one creates anew in the moment, without reference to the past or the future. In this metaphor of surfing the wave and staying over your feet, we are talking about staying rooted where you ARE—in the present moment—rather than in the "past" (where you have been) or the "future" (where you are going). If you think about it, all fear derives from past experience being projected onto the future. When things arise in your present moment that remind you of something from the past, you can easily project that the past experience will repeat itself in the moments that follow the time of remembering that past. This is when you feel fear. It's inner talk that says, "It was like this before, so it will be like this again." If you experienced pain in the past, you expect it will be painful again. That is where the fear comes in. You want to avoid the pain. "I'm afraid that if this moment goes the way it went before, I'll experience what I experienced before, and I don't want to do that again."

The answer to this is to cut through the cords of memory, to interrupt the inner talk by saying out loud, "That was then. This is now." Boom! You are back in the present, able to choose anew in the present moment. When you say the word "now," you bring your attention into the present. Say "NOW" out loud, right now. Feel NOW. What is really happening NOW? Not what happened before, not what MIGHT happen later. What is really happening NOW? Do you see how you are in the habit of scaring yourself? Cultivate the practice of living NOW. Live each moment as the only moment that exists. That is how it will be on Terra. Get used to it. Create a little bit of Terra right where you are, NOW. NOW is the only place you can create anything. NOW is the only place you can choose anything. NOW is all you ever really have.

When we say the word "moment," it will be useful to define what we mean. A moment is an "event" that arises from the matrix of Infinite Mind. It contains everything within it for its natural fulfillment and completion. It is not measured by minutes, seconds, or hours. It is a unit of experience that may be very short or go on for some time. You can FEEL when a moment begins. You can FEEL when it completes. Every moment has a beginning, a middle, and a conclusion, like a phrase in speech or music. Think of it entering into your field of awareness, swelling into its fullness, and then receding as it completes. There is a wavelike quality to a moment. A wave emerges from the ocean, swells, moves forward, and then resolves back into the ocean. Just so with a moment. It emerges from the ocean of consciousness that is the Mind of the Creator. It swells upward into your perceptual field, and moves forward, then ebbs from your experience as it completes. There is background and foreground, and there are different waves overlapping. In the past, you were only peripherally aware of the background, as your attention was captured by the foreground, but now your senses will be broadened and deepened until you are like a bowl containing ALL of it—all of the ocean and all of the waves upon its surface. You will be aware of all of it simultaneously and be able to move your attention to whatever you feel called to pay attention to, at will.

This is a natural expansion of your consciousness into full consciousness. As your consciousness expands, it will affect everything else—your body, your surroundings, the quality of your interaction with your environment. You will begin to merge with the Mind of the Creator. You will experience the peace and serenity, the infinite spaciousness of that, and you will become that peace; you will become that spaciousness that is vast enough to hold it all within you—in love and without judgment. That is where you are going. That is the experience you are moving into, even now. As you move forward within time, you will gradually stop caring about where you are going and when. The chatter and the impatience will simply fall away. You will feel when something is no longer appropriate for you—whether it is the clamor of the media, the noise of deepening conflict, or anything else that is not in keeping with this deep sense of peace and infinite space. When this occurs, simply let go and let God. Let the peace and spaciousness of the Creator become your field of play. Let go of anything that does not belong in that space. You don't have to engage in conflict. You can simply let go of your resistance, of your attachments to being "right" or "better than." You can simply let go and let God. Let everyone do the same for themselves. If people have attachments to their way of seeing and being, allow them to remain that way. They will receive what is perfect for them, also. This is an "operation" based in love and respect for all choices. Be responsible for YOUR choices, and let everyone else have the same privilege.

We shall speak to you again on this topic. Amen, Adonoy Sabayoth. We are the Hosts of Heaven.

"As you are leaving the world you have known, you are also approaching a new world, the world of your dreams. As you are closing off those ties to those whom you have known, you are also opening up to make new associations, with those who are more closely aligned with your particular path and destination. It is a grand sorting out that is taking place and there are both sorrows and joys to be found along the way."

ASCENSION IS A PROCESS, PART THREE
November 26, 2001

All right, now. We have asked to speak to you today in this, our final discourse on this particular topic, so that we may both come to closure on THIS topic and lay the foundation for that which follows. You see, that is the way things work in the Creation. Every ending is also a beginning. Every closure is also an opening, and so it is with our work with you and so it is with your ascension process, as well.

As you are leaving the world you have known, you are also approaching a new world, the world of your dreams. As you are closing off those ties to those whom you have known, you are also opening up to make new associations, with those who are more closely aligned with your particular path and destination. It is a grand sorting out that is taking place and there are both sorrows and joys to be found along the way. We hope to bring you more of the latter than the former, so please bear with us as we enter this new territory together.

First of all, please take note of the fact that there are three parts to this discourse. There will be three volumes in this material before we are through, and that is no accident. Every number is a symbol for a particular energy configuration and certain numbers are called prime numbers and have special significance, as they form the foundation for other numbers. They also reflect and embody a certain aspect of the design of Creation, and they are used in describing that design. There are also certain geometries involved that are a reflection of "how things work" in a particular Creation—the outpicturing of certain dynamics there are inherent in that Creation and in keeping with its Universal Laws.

We will not attempt to give you a comprehensive treatise on these subjects, for our topic today is the subject of ascension, so we will only make mention of those aspects of these things that relate to our topic —your ascension process. Many of you have read and use some terms interchangeably, such as dimension and density, which from our perspective is not an accurate thing and leads to some confusion. We hope to clarify those things also, as it all relates to your understanding of who you really are, and how you project yourself into your many different forms.

To begin with, you are a projection from Source. The Original Thought became manifest as a projection of that Thought. All of you who are bound for Terra are part of that Original Thought. You are the first generation of Creation and are creators yourselves. But who and what is this Creator who does the thinking? And how are you related to It? You have words such as "ineffable" to express the nature of the Creator. You also use other words, such as omnipresent, omniscient, omnipotent, etc. for the same purpose. Ineffable means "unknowable; incapable of being described; incapable of being grasped/understood." It is considered to be an attribute of the Creator. All those other words are attributes, also. They describe aspects or qualities of the Creator. So, to your limited frame of reference, the nature of the Creator is beyond your capacity to understand, beyond your ability to comprehend. And perhaps that is true for you NOW, but when you have crossed the threshold, you will EXPERIENCE the Creator directly. You will experience your true connection with and relationship to the Creator, and then you will truly be "home." Then you will have no more need of words to describe what cannot be described. You will simply EXIST in that relationship and knowing.

Now, who is this "you" we are talking about? You are a projection of that Creator, a product of that Creator's Thought, and you exist only in the Mind of the Creator. All of Creation exists only in the Mind of the Creator. It is Thought made manifest through the medium of light and sound. Sound is the word you use to describe vibration, which is the oscillation between two opposing states. Your entire reality is oscillating between two opposing states—"on" and "off." You reality is only "there" half of the time, but the oscillations are so rapid that you perceive of things as being continuous, as being constantly "on." But in reality, the Creation is being re-created over and over again—"refreshed" or "redrawn" over and over again, many times a second. So "you" only exist half of the time, yourselves! Where are you during the other half of the time? You ARE the Creator at rest. Think about it. You ARE the Creator at rest. There is a spectrum of vibration involved, and the only difference is the speed at which the oscillations take place.

We have spoken of the "inbreath" and "outbreath" of the Creator, which is measured in billions of your years. That is one cycle of Creation. At the other end of the spectrum is this very rapid cycling, this very rapid alternation between "on" and "off" that makes up your physical reality—or rather that which APPEARS to be your physical reality. It is all a projection, and the Creator is the "projector" of the entire Creation, including you. You are players in the Creator's "movie," only instead of a single, static "screen" in a movie house, the Creator gets to view its Creation through the perceptual screens of each and every aspect of Its Creation—an infinitude of perceptions, all streaming back into the Creator from Its projections.

The Creator exists as an infinitely vast field of intelligent energy, and the first generation—the Elohim—are only slightly less so. They are extremely vast also, but are a single step removed from absolute infinitude. They do have boundary and identity. You are the expression or projection of one of the Elohim. You are among those who came together to project this portion of the Creation from within your being, so many billions of years ago. But your projection does not just consist of this level of being that you presently experience as your physical reality. It has many levels—many different frequency bands—that make up a continuous spectrum of reality, not unlike the spectrum of light and sound that makes up the Creation itself.

You exist simultaneously on all of the levels or frequency bands that exist. You exist as vast fields of intelligent energy and you exist as single points of pure consciousness and light without form—simultaneously. You exist as embodiments or expressions across the entire frequency spectrum, also, and all of your expressions exist simultaneously with each other. Right now, your attention is placed within the locus of your physical expression on Earth, but as your ascension proceeds, you will be accessing more and more of your other levels of being, also. You will be defining yourself quite differently, and you will be changing in many ways, to more properly express your chosen level of being for a given time and place.

These Messages are being given in a series, in a sequence, proceeding from the outer or more superficial aspects toward the core or more central aspects of our discussion. It is all about the journey back to your true Selves, toward remembering who you really are and toward regaining your true powers and true nature of expression. It is hard for you to imagine how much and how little CHOICE there is available to you. You see, when you have so little comprehension of your true place in things, you are like a blind person, guessing at what lies around you. You have so MUCH choice because the possible choices are nearly infinite. You have so LITTLE choice, because there is only ONE right choice for you in a given moment. When you are fully conscious of your nature and connection with Source, you will be at peace and at rest within both of those seeming paradoxes: the fact that there are so many choices available and the fact that there is only ONE "right" choice for you to make—one choice that is wholly in keeping with who you are and where you fit within the relationship between all of the other expressions of the Creator with which you interact.

So you exist on Earth, in your physical bodies, but you also exist at other levels at the same time. You exist in all the other frequency bands, as well, and each frequency band has its own "laws" that govern form and function within that band. Most of you who are reading these Messages are going to go to Terra and will express in forms and have functions that are appropriate to that frequency band—that density of the Creation. AT THE SAME TIME, you will continue to exist at all of the other frequency bands, and you will be able to choose where you put your attention—through which frequency band you perceive. You will be aware of your "other selves," but the one "right" focus will be your primary one, with all of the others existing as a backdrop of potentials that is always available to you. Some of you will relate to Terra from other platforms, to oversee and guide those upon her surface, as those are the roles that you have chosen for that experience, also. At all times, all of you will be existing at all of your levels at once, but one locus will be primary. You will be a focus of attention in one particular part of the vast ocean of Cosmic Mind, aware of the rest as a constant backdrop for your experience.

We have spoken of the holographic model. All things are contained as potentials within the hologram. This is what we mean by this backdrop. It is made up of all the potentials. In full consciousness, you will experience the presence of all the potentials at the same time as you experience the focus of the EXPRESSION of ONE of those potentials. We will speak more on this topic at another time, but we just want to give you a little look at this idea, now. You will be aware of ALL of it while expressing just one choice within it at any given time.

Now to the subject of numbers. There are essences that are expressed by numbers, and prime numbers can be said to be prime essences, like what you might think of when you think of primary colors. Your primary colors of visible light are red, green, and blue. All other colors are made up of those 3 colors, in combination with intensity or lack of it. When you blend these 3 colors in varying proportions and intensity, you get all of the other colors, including the extremes of pure white (the complete presence of all 3 colors in equal proportions and at full intensity) and pure black (the ABSENCE of all color and the point of zero intensity). Numbers act in similar ways, but with far more complexity. Numbers are symbolic distillations of the essence of certain properties, and primary numbers cannot be further reduced. They are foundational. All numbers that are NOT primary numbers are made up of combinations of various primary numbers, and can be "taken apart" into their primary components.

What does all of this talk about numbers and colors have to do with your ascension process? It is to give you a grasp of ESSENCE, of FOUNDATION, of ROOT or GROUND. You are returning to your essence, to that primary expression of your being, independent of your expression in a particular environment. Your essence is your primary color, your primary sound, your primary quality. It is the thing that is the "true you," independent of any incarnational expression. It is the pure vibrational pattern that is your particular configuration and there are only so many of those available within a given spectrum of Creation. All the rest are made up of combinations and alterations of that primary configuration. To be in full consciousness means to KNOW your essence. And not only will you know your own essence, you will also recognize the essence of others.

There have been some individuals in human history on your planet who embodied this kind of understanding and modeled it for others. Now all of you who are going to Terra will be embodying your essence. You are dropping all that is NOT in keeping with your essence, and you are filling yourselves with more and more of your essential nature as this process proceeds. The questions of intellect fall away in the fullness of your experience of your essence. You are filled with the peace of knowing who you are, where your place is in the Creation, and of knowing what is your one "right" choice in any given moment. All struggle is gone. All doubt is gone. All there is left is the peace and the quiet joy of knowing at last the answers to those questions that have formed the basis of your seeking through all these billions of years. You will simply KNOW, and you will never again have to forget what you know, ever again.

We will speak more about these numbers, colors, and higher aspects of the Creation at other times. For now, we wish you to simply know where this is heading. When your transformation is complete, you will simply KNOW who you are, where you fit within all of this, how you relate to the Creator Itself, and what is "right action" or "right choice" in any given moment. You can begin to practice that now, though, by simply remaining quiet enough to hear the "voice within." In the midst of the tumult and the noise around you, you can listen instead to the silence and the voice within. In each and every moment, you can choose peace instead of struggle and conflict. You can walk away from those people and those experiences that scream for you to ease their pain by engulf-ing you in it. You can bring peace to others only if you can embody it yourself. You can bring peace only if you ARE at peace within yourself. As long as you are striving within yourself, toward some imagined outcome, you are not at peace. Peace, peace, peace. That is the "pearl of great price." Be peace. Be at peace. Be peace.

We leave you now in peace and honor and blessing. One day, you will be like us again, too. Amen, Adonoy Sabayoth. We are the Hosts of Heaven.

I have received several queries about the reference to the primary colors, so I wanted to clear up the apparent confusion. The primary colors of LIGHT are red, green, and blue, and they are the ones that create the images on your TV sets and computer monitors. The primary colors of PIGMENTS, such as ink, dyes and paint, and the pigments in skin, hair, and eyes are identified as cyan, magenta, and yellow. Light works differently than pigments do.

When you combine LIGHT colors, they are ADDITIVE and RADIANT. The more intense and the greater quantity of each color, the lighter and brighter they get. Light creates colors as it passes through transparent media, such as glass, gels, and transparent plastics. When you combine all three primary colors of LIGHT in equal proportions and at full intensity, you get WHITE light.

When you combine PIGMENT colors, they are SUBTRACTIVE. Each pigment ABSORBS all color except its own, which it reflects back to you. The total absence of light (i.e. all color is absorbed and none is being radiated back at you) is perceived as black. When you combine all three primary colors of PIGMENTS, you get various shades of "black/grey," according to the absorbent capacity of the particular pigments used. The "black" you see in black cats is really a very dark brown, which absorbs nearly all the light that hits it. Pigments are made up of substances that subtract everything from the light reflecting off the surface except the color you see. They are used for "reflective" media, such as paper, canvas, and cloth.

The familiar "primary colors" that you were taught about in

school (red, blue, and yellow) are made up of pigments that, when mixed, make up the complementary colors of orange, purple, and green. That is yet another color system. It is based on what happens when you mix particular pigments with each other. What is important to understand about that system is that it is still a subtractive system, and the colors that are reflected back to your eye are still mixtures of the primary subtractive colors—cyan, magenta, and yellow.

This Message is talking about the primary colors of LIGHT, not those of pigments. White light contains all colors, and when it is passed through a prism, you see all the colors of visible light, from red through violet. Our chakras are based on the LIGHT colors, not the PIGMENT colors. The middle chakra of the 7 body chakras is the heart chakra and its color is GREEN. The lower 3 chakras are red, orange and yellow (note that yellow is not in the middle), and the upper 3 chakras are blue, indigo, and violet—all together they make up the colors of the rainbow, the visible light spectrum. I hope this is helpful to you in understanding this Message.

Peace and blessings,
Lyara

IT'S BOOSTER ROCKET TIME!
January 2, 2002

All right, now. We have several things to say to you today, on both the near and more distant view. The closest thing to you on the time horizon is a somewhat massive event that will mark the separating out of the different realities from one another to such an extent that they will begin to experience events that are not shared with all of the other realities that will emerge. This event will be felt in every corner of the world as a very deep shock, and one that will rouse even the most deeply slumbering individuals to a dawning realization that the world will not ever be the same again.

The events that have preceded this forthcoming shock were relatively mild compared to what comes now and what will follow it in relatively rapid succession. You are nearly at the threshold of the parting of the ways and this will become more obvious to you in hindsight, after sufficient time has passed that you can look back and see a pattern. To put this in a proper context, we wish to make use of a scientifically observed process as a metaphor for what is about to occur. As with all metaphors, there is an oversimplification of a complex situation, but it will serve to illustrate our point well enough for you to make it the rest of the way on your own.

When a living cell is going to divide, a number of things occur. In the resting stage, the chromatin—those threads of DNA that carry the genetic information of the cell and the organism—are loosely spread throughout the nucleus of the cell, making it difficult to determine just where one thread leaves off and another begins. However, when the time nears for the cell to divide itself into two separate halves, the chromatin begin bunching up and separating out from the other threads so that they form distinct chromosomes that can be observed as such under the microscope. Then they replicate and the two identical pairs line up along the equatorial plate in the cell, which will become the plane of division when the process completes. Meanwhile, the "poles" of the cell have migrated so that they are opposite each other and at right angles to the equatorial plate, not very different from the relationship between the poles and the equator on your physical planet. Fine threads from the center of each chromosome attach to these poles (one from each pair goes to one of the poles; the other one of the pair attaches to the other pole) and when all is lined up, the cell pinches inward at the equator and divides.

In this process, things go along fairly slowly at first, but when all is finally lined up, the process completes rather quickly. So it is with you right now, in your planetary process. It has been a relatively slow process of sorting out into your groups and aligning with your poles of destiny, but this next event will be the "shot heard 'round the world," and it will mark the "beginning of the end"—that point at which the different realities physically move away from each other toward their "poles of destiny." In other words, despite that fact that you can look back on your previous year as a time of increasing acceleration—particularly from September onward—once this event occurs, things will kick into high gear and much will follow in rapid succession, just as the cell rapidly separates into its new "daughter cells" and they then move apart from each other and journey separately from that point on.

A cell only splits into two cells, and there will be several different realities that split off from each other in this process, but the key point to grasp here is the significance of this next event in terms of marking the beginning of this actual movement into separate realities, and to prepare yourself for the speed at which things will unfold after that. Despite the shock of September and some of the things that happened afterward, the last few weeks have been pretty tame compared to what is coming next and afterward. We encourage you to keep your breath open, to remain detached while observing all of this occurring, and to realize that for those who are headed toward Terra, this could be considered the "booster rocket" for your journey in that direction. There is no one who will not FEEL this impact, but there are many ways of perceiving it. If you were strapped into the seat of a space shuttle and the rockets kicked in under you, you would feel that impact and acceleration, but you would know that it was taking you upward toward your destination and mission. You may choose the same response to this next shock on your perceptual screen, and it would be good if you can do that. Instead of viewing it as a disaster, many of you will be able to say, "Finally! We are under way."

Many of you who are reading this have been "on your way" for a long time, and have experienced many shifts in your understanding and perceptions. Now, however, the time of learning and processing will change from dealing with those things of the past toward dealing with those things that are now coming into your life. Many of you are still in the process of leaving old relationships and circumstances. That may continue for awhile for some of you, but most of you will find the rate of change in your life to be exhilarating and experience more and more joy in the journey as you begin to experience the rush of freedom, as you let go of those things and people who hold you back. You remember an old title—Inherit the Wind? You will inherit the wind. You will become accustomed to streaming like the wind, to be moving so fast it brings tears to your eyes, but they will be tears of joy that you are finally underway and can feel the movement as you stream toward your destination.

Others will be experiencing rapid change, also, but it will not bring them joy—in part because they will be losing a lot of what they are very attached to: pictures of reality that must change in the face of the events that will come now, ways of being that will no longer be possible. Many things taken for granted will pass away, and those who can move through these times with grace and surrender will experience wonder and awe at the unfolding. People will look at the ashes of their past and some will understand that it clears the way for a new beginning, while others will sort through the ashes, trying to recover something remembered to take with them—to take with them what no longer has life in an effort to hold onto that life which is gone.

It is easy to point fingers of blame, but as we have said before, when you get down to the core, you must blame the Creator who has created all that you see and feel. It is all "good" to the Creator because it fulfills the purpose of the Creation—to provide experiences for the Creator to enjoy through Its creations. This shock that comes is all part of the larger exit plan for the Creation. Nothing will be left of the old world when it is done. Everyone will be gone from the present planet, through one exit path or another. Everyone will experience continuity in their perceived reality, but this event will mark the time when not everyone experiences the SAME reality. If you could compare notes, you would discover that different people experience different things, and this will increase as you move through time to the finale of the drama of 3D Earth.

As things move forward, you will see your destination more and more clearly by virtue of its contrast with everything else that is going on. Likewise, other people with other destinations will perceive THOSE more clearly, so it will seem like everyone else that does not share one's particular views is mistaken, but this movement will accommodate them all, in one way or another.

So, for example, if you hear that a large planet or comet is coming that will result in a pole shift or cataclysms in 2003, that is a perception that belongs to a particular exit path, and you simply allow those people who perceive that to do so. That path is not "yours," and it does not lead to Terra, so all you need to be concerned with is the path that IS "yours" and to follow what presents in your life that will lead you further in that direction. There has been much talk in the past of many scenarios that have not manifested—mass landings, the Photon Belt, etc. However, now the many paths that are being "seen" by those who can "see" in that way have a greater likelihood of coming to pass. Even the scenarios that are put forth by the deceivers will come to pass for some people in some way, because thought creates and if enough people believe in a particular outcome, their combined thoughts will manifest that reality. That is why we are sharing these Messages with you—so that those who are coded to respond and can feel that response will add their energies with others of like mind and heart and will manifest that which we speak of to you.

It is a paradox that Terra already exists and yet you have to align with it for it to manifest for you. It is a reciprocal relationship, like a mirror of sorts. Terra calls to you, and you seek Terra. In the aligning with the vision, it is a little like a "lock" in a missile guidance system. In reading these Messages, you "lock" onto the "target" of Terra, and Terra attracts you by her presence in your perceptual field. Not everyone is this way, and though it might seem like you are alone in your perceptions when compared with those around you, consider that there are nearly 6 million of you altogether and you will have a LOT of company once you are all together again. You have been together before, in groupings of various sizes and at various historical times and places, but now the time is coming when you will all be together at once, in one place again, before you are complete and depart for your other journeys on the way back to Source and your final dissolution as a separate being.

Those of you who are going to Terra will be there long enough to establish the colonies and bear your children, and then you will be off to other adventures in the cosmos. For the next century plus [some years], your focus will be Terra, but then you will be through with that and will move on. That is the nature of things. One exploration leads to the next, and that next one leads to the next one after that, infinitely. Terra calls you now, and she is your safe harbor from the storm that now comes. Remember that. The storms that come now are the booster rockets lifting you toward your dream of a world without storms, without wars, without death, and if you miss the thunder and lightning, you will be able to travel to wilder places to visit with that, too, but Terra and her peace will be your home for the rest of your present incarnation. When it is time to leave, you will simply change form and move on. No pain. No death. No sorrow again, ever. Now THAT will be a welcome thing, won't it? We look forward to having you amongst us again.

We leave you now, in peace and honor and blessing. Amen, Adonoy Sabayoth. We are the Hosts of Heaven.

ON YOUR WAY HOME
February 22, 2002

All right, now. We have asked to speak to you tonight because something very wonderful is looming on your horizon. It is not what you would expect, but it is still wonderful from our perspective. A grand awakening is about to take place and for you who have been patiently waiting for release from the world of so much sorrow, this will mark the true beginning of the final stage of your departure from this world, on the way to the next.

We have spoken before of this event. It is a global wakeup call, so that everyone, everywhere in the world can know something has fundamentally and irrevocably changed. For some change is and can be terrifying, but change can also be seen as good news, too. We encourage you to embrace change in this way—as good news to be celebrated, as the "beginning of the end" of this sorrow. If you can see it this way, then you can quietly rejoice in your heart with the sure knowing of what follows. Despite appearances, it is truly good news—an end to the suffering of this world, an end to the pain of this world, once and for all, forever. This is what is in store for you—total joy, total love, total peace.

But on the way to that joy and peace there is a period of upheaval as part of this massive change. It is for this reason that we have spent so much time and energy in preparing you for this time and these occurrences. If you can but keep your eyes on the far horizon, where that new world awaits you in all of her radiance and joy, then you will pass through this time with less attention on what is passing away and more attention on where you are headed through the times ahead.

We wish you to know, also, that we are always with you. If we do not speak to you through these words, we speak to you through our silence. Silence is a Message, too. It says, "Listen within." It says, "Pay attention to what feelings come up when the Hosts have not spoken for awhile." Do you get anxious to hear from us? Then seek our comfort within. If our beloved messenger were suddenly plucked from your midst, what would you do? Find us and our comfort within. When you stop grasping at the fragile comforts that make up your external world, you can experience the richness and the comforts of your inner world. If you focus on what you DON'T have, you will never realize how much you DO have. That is one of the reasons we have encouraged you to live your life with appreciation. By doing that, you fill yourself every minute of every day and you are truly wealthy in the things that matter most.

Now that we have put our gloss on the story, let us acknowledge that not everyone will see things the way you do. You must understand this and not get caught up in the maelstrom that is soon to surround you. There will be a great deal of confusion, anger, and fear, and these things will be exploited by those who profit from them. Do not get caught up in the drama. Remember our counsel to seek the peace of deep ocean? Remember it when these times are upon you. Let the events flow around you, but maintain a place of calm trust and serenity within you. These events will be the harbinger of even more intense times, but carry your peace with you like a shield and you will weather the storms well.

Please note that we are now speaking in the plural. There is not one single event, but a entire panorama of events of all kinds and types that will constitute the face of change in your world. They will be everywhere you look, and once it dawns on people that there is some possible connection from one to another, they will be roused from their sleep in a most unpleasant way. You are not sleeping. You are already awakening and you have within you the means to create peace and safety for yourself and your loved ones, be they human or otherwise. Peace is an attitude, not something you can buy at a store already packaged. To be sure, you can read books and listen to soothing music, but even those actions are an expression of an ATTITUDE of SEEKING peace. Seek peace. Be peace. Be humble in your seeking and let go of the clinging to the comforts you used to seek. Open to receive the comforts that count, the ones that have no price because they are priceless. Peace, peace, peace. It is your sanctuary through the storm. Peace, peace, peace. It is the savior of your soul, your sanity, your hearts and minds. Seek peace in the midst of the storm.

If choices come (and they will), make the choice for peace. As the frequencies rise, everything that is a symptom of the malaise of this world will surface. Peace heals. Be at peace. Drop the struggle to hold on. In letting go, you gain more than you lose. Some of you will find it harder to do this than others, but we assure you that you have created yourself with the necessary reserves, the necessary heart, the necessary strength to do this, and in so doing, you will rejoice even more because of the discovery that you are thriving in the midst of the storms. You will thrive because you are made for these times.

You have found your homing beacon in these Messages and you carry within you the map and the compass for the journey. Even if we were silent, you would find your way home. Be peace. Be at peace. You are on your way now, and nothing will stop you from making the trip home. You are coming home to yourself, to the world of your dreams, and to each other. In light of all that, what does it matter if the old shell cracks and shatters? When it's time for the chick to come out of the egg, the shell has to crack and shatter. You are coming out of your shell. The world will crack and shatter around you and you will be coming home. Focus on the journey ahead, rather than what you leave behind. Let everyone make their own decisions now, as the grouping around the poles of destiny is taking place more and more each day. There are many partings to take place on the road ahead and many who are still in your life may pass from your view, but you are coming home. Your animals, your loved ones, everyone whom you love will be provided for, in keeping with their life plan. You can trust the process. You can trust the journey. You are coming home.

If we are silent sometimes, it is so that you can learn to listen to your own sound, to your own inner voice instead of ours. We are family, you and we, and we are here with you every step of the way. But we do not wish you to become dependent on hearing our voice to know you are safe and loved. We wish you to hear your own inner voice to know you are safe and loved. Go within. Meditate. Breathe. Feel the calm and peace you can create when you can remember to breathe. As things get more intense around you, find ways to feel calmer and more relaxed. Take a hot bath. Go for a walk. Listen to sounds that soothe you—streams, rivers, the sighing of the wind in the trees, a gentle rain. You can even get recordings of these sounds if you want, so you can create this experience for yourself whenever you need to remind yourself that what is going on around you is not all there is to the picture. Be good to yourself. Cherish yourself for the beautiful being that you are. The long lonely walk is far shorter now than it was and you are on your way home. Remember that. You are on your way home.

Amen, Adonoy Sabayoth. We are the Hosts of Heaven.

THE "GOD GAME"
April 9, 2002

For those who have eyes to see, it is evident that much change is going on all around you. Yet, if you follow our instructions, you can deepen your sense of peace and calm and remain serene, even as things accelerate and intensify. The threshold event of which we have spoken is still some time off in your future, and we would hope that with this long lead time to reflect and prepare, you will have integrated the necessary understanding to respond to it with quiet acceptance, knowing that it brings with it the final stages of your exit from planet Earth and the beginnings of the new world that follows.

Yet we also know how much you love to hear from us and how it helps you to hear our perspective on things, so in the spirit of an interlude, we thought we would entertain you a bit with our discourse today. Our model indeed comes from your world of entertainment, although we hope that you will take away something a bit deeper than just that. Sometimes entertainment can be an easy way to swallow what would otherwise be bitter medicine, and we hope that will be the case today.

If life is viewed as a sort of movie, with everyone playing their part and speaking their lines, then God/the Creator is the ultimate filmmaker. We have spoken before of the Oversoul and how it creates the simultaneous projections of itself—what you experience as your embodiments or "lives." The Oversoul is the projector

111

for those individual expressions of itself and God/the Creator is the scriptwriter for all of the movies that play out through the Oversouls, regardless of their polarity. As we have often said, the Creator has created EVERYTHING in order to experience Itself through Its creations. We have also commented on how it was necessary to create the two polarities in order to increase the potential for increasingly complex experiences, and how the Oversouls themselves come in two "flavors" or polarities, which we have identified as the STS (service to self) and STO (service to others) orientation.

In movies, there are opposing forces and conflict, and it is also true in the "movie" of life. Think about that for a moment. If you went to see a movie and everything was harmonious and smooth, you would find it rather flat and uninteresting after a very short while. There would be no challenges to overcome, nothing but a kind of pleasant sameness and not much going on at any time. Not much stimulation, and your mind would become restless and begin contemplating other things. That's because you want your movies to be entertainment, and for that reason they need opposing forces, conflict and challenges to be overcome. And so it is with 3D life. If there were not enough stimulus, people would lapse into a sort of lethargy and boredom and lose interest or have to manufacture situations where they could experience intensity and variety. Such is the nature of the one who seeks to ever know more. And the Creator's chief desire is always to know more of Itself through the interaction of Its creations. We will call this aspect of the Creator's creative play "The God Game." In the God Game, the Creator "wears" all of Its creations and plays all of the "parts" (roles/characters) through all of Its created parts.

At the higher densities, the game changes, the rules change, but it is still the God Game at its core. Now, what does this have to do with anything and how can this be of help in understanding what you experience from day to day and over time? Well, in the God Game, every one of you who is reading this is a character in the movie. Characters have personality traits they are born with, and they have traits that are learned through their experiences. In 3D, the catalyst is pain. In 4D, the catalyst is love. You are in 3D and your character has been shaped by your pain and by your seeking. Most of your defining moments—those moments in which an experience affected you so deeply that it changed the course of your life—involved your pain and/or your seeking. Your seeking comes from the Creator's desire to know Itself through Its creations. Your pain comes from the Creator's desire to know Itself through Its creations. The Creator desires to know more about Itself, so the catalyst for all experiences are both the seeking and the pain.

Now, how are those conditions to be met? What will provide the pain and what will support the seeking? You can view the sources of pain as "enemies" or "perpetrators" or STS "villains" if you want. Those labels are used to identify sources of pain in your life. But they are as needed for the fullness of your experience in 3D as are the sources of support for your seeking—those whom you would call "friends" or "loved ones" or "teachers." Both are needed for the fullness of your experience and for the entire script or drama to play out. Both of those are the Creator expressing through Its creations, through the God Game. Here is a little insight into how it goes:

The pure Light of Creation, conditioned by Love as an ordering force, streams endlessly from the Source/Creator through the lenses of the Oversouls. The Oversouls color the light with their own particular biases or "angle of perception/reception" and the Light takes on a particular quality from having passed through the Oversoul. You could view these qualities as archetypes, as biases, or as themes to be explored. We like to view them as essences. In their purest state, they are the essence of a particular aspect of the Creator, and there are many of them available. We may explore this concept further at a future time, but for now, just understand that each Oversoul exists to explore a particular essence or theme, and it will do so by creating "lives" in many different settings or environments. However, all of the OTHER Oversouls are doing the same thing, so in any given environment, one has the presence and potential for interaction with many different essences, and this provides a rich basis for many different kinds of experiences. For all practical purposes, the original set of possibilities was infinite, but now many (if not most) of those possibilities have been explored and there is a distillation going on, back into the original essence.

In the world around you, every person you see is going through a process of this distillation back into the original essence. They are becoming MORE of who they really are. This can cause some problems when a person was really just accommodating the expectations of those around them or living their life as a reaction to their defining moments. There is a lot of rejection of past hurts going on and a lot of intensified seeking. What a glorious time to be in a body! At no time in the history of planet Earth has there been such a rich potential for intensified experience. How much more interesting the movie is from the Creator's perspective! In the God Game, the more intense the experience, the better it is for the richness that it provides.

Let's now look at some examples. If the focus of the exploration is the theme of power, then there is the potential to explore both the absence of power (powerlessness) and the possession of power. In the absence of power, one also learns about the possession of power from those who have power over them, and the reverse is true for the person who possesses the power—they learn from those whom they have the power over. There is a RECIPROCITY that is inherent in the God Game. God supplies all of the needed players and is both teaching and learning at the same time. Each player is a teacher for the other and is also learning from the other. Each person is a mirror for the other one to see himself/herself more clearly, to know himself/herself more deeply. After many lifetimes have been created and experienced, all of this teaching and learning becomes integrated into the collective experience of the Oversoul, and thence back to the Creator. It all comes from the INTERACTION of the particular Oversoul's projections with the projections of the OTHER Oversouls. This is how the Creator can experience Itself through Its Creations. The experience of one particular Oversoul is amplified, enriched, and colored by the interaction with the projections from the other Oversouls. And it is a totally dynamic process, with feedback and alteration at each node of interaction. In fact, this is not just true of people, but of the entire fabric of the created or manifest worlds.

Your scientists have discovered a fundamental building block of matter, which they have called a quark. A quark is made out of Light. Not light as illumination, but Light that is a substance. ALL matter is built up of these units of Light. Now, these quarks are made out of Light, but they are shaped or conditioned by vibration, or Sound. Together, Sound and Light form the material ground for the manifest worlds. But there is one more aspect to consider. When a quark interacts with another quark, they are BOTH CHANGED by the interaction. So even at the most fundamental level of material expression, a dynamic process of constant interaction and change is going on. What's more, there is an underlying field of consciousness or awareness that is the matrix for the entire collection of all of the quarks that are carrying on these interactions. So, at the most fundamental level, all quarks are interconnected with all other quarks by being contained in this field of conscious awareness. This field is the Mind of God. All manifest reality is embedded in the Mind of God and is interconnected through the matrix of the Mind of God. When you say "All things are connected," this is a fundamental truth.

The Oversouls are vast fields of intelligent energy. They are self-aware, and yet, they too, are embedded in the same matrix. When they project their projections, they manifest them through the quarks that are the building blocks of matter. All things, all manifestations, both from the level of the projector—the Oversoul—and the particles that make up the manifestation of the Oversoul's projection are embedded in the Mind of God. Therefore, in the God Game, God is experiencing Itself as both the filmmaker and the actors in the movie that It makes. These actors are not just people. They are also things like the wind and rain, flowers and trees, insects and animals. They are all the creations of the Creator. They are all players in the God Game. They are all sources of catalyst for pain and for the support of one's seeking.

Take a rock, for example. If you stub your toe on a rock or step on a sharp stone with your bare foot, it can provide you with the experience of pain. But another rock could offer you a foothold when you are climbing up a steep trail or wanting to cross a stream. They're all rocks, and they are all part of the God Game. If your life script requires you to cross a stream at some point in your seeking, the rock is an element of your experience. The rock is also sentient and it experiences you stepping on it. It experiences your energy, your thoughts, and it experiences the feeling of weight or pressure from being stepped on. The rock is experiencing, too.

Now, take a look at some of the things that are going on in your world today. A major portion of the Ross Ice Shelf collapsed in the Antarctic recently, a part of the changes that are going on. This change was a result of other changes that had already occurred. When those huge blocks of ice are set free to float and eventually melt, they affect the oceans that they float in. The fresh water from the melting ice changes the salinity of the water around them. That change in the salinity produces a subtle change in the flow of the ocean's currents. That change in the flow of the ocean's currents produces a subtle change in the weather patterns. Those changes in the weather patterns affect crops and food production. That change in food production affects the availability of food and also of prices for those foods. Those changes in availability and pricing produce other subtle changes, such as a subtle alteration of people's priorities. When people are starving, they become desperate to survive at all costs, and that leads them to act in ways that they would not otherwise act. Those actions in turn affect other things which set in motion still other things, and so the God Game goes. Every single part of the manifest worlds affects every other part of the manifest worlds. It is all connected through the Mind of God, and God is everywhere that anything exists. It is all part of the God Game, wherein God interacts with Itself through Its creations.

With the return to essence, with things (and especially people) becoming more of what they really are underneath their conditioning and environmental pressures, you see many things surfacing. Polarization increases as the heroes and the villains become more like their true essence. Positive becomes more positive. Negative becomes more negative. Things that one took on from others and which are not part of their essence become cast off, sometimes in unpleasant ways. Body aches and pains, emotional aches and pains, spiritual aches and pains—all of these are part of the purification of essence that is going on. Tolerance is lower for those things that are not compatible with one's essence. There is a greater tendency to withdraw from what is not compatible with one's essence, and that is seen as the great sorting out into all of the groupings, which we have spoken about before. There are things surfacing that come as surprises at times, to find that one is not the person one thought they were. Much of what has shaped your self-perception is the result of those early experiences in life—those defining experiences that set you off on a particular course, exploring particular options, attempting to heal your pain, attempting to define your seeking and find what it is you seek.

So if you find your life changing now, in fundamental ways, it is because the God Game is nearly over for this chapter in the Creation story. God has explored the themes, the roles, the potentials that were available through the parameters of this particular environment, and as in every good movie, it is time for the final act, where the question gets answered, the conflicts are resolved, and everyone goes off to live in the sequel! Your sequel is life on the ships and then life on Terra—a trilogy, if you like, and one that will still be just an interlude on the way to other movies. You are coming home. You are becoming more of your essence. You are beginning to know who the "others" are whom you want to be with. And none of this would be possible without the God Game. None of this would be possible without the protagonists and the antagonists, without the heroes and the villains. Every script requires both for the story to move forward. Conflict leads to resolution and in that resolution, everyone is changed by the interaction. Change is eternal. You are eternal, and you will eternally change.

We leave you now in peace, honor and blessing. Amen, Adonoy Sabayoth. We are the Hosts of Heaven.

We cannot emphasize too much that it is important to remain detached and to not get caught up in the drama that is unfolding all around you. The moment you engage with chaos, you get sucked into it. The moment you polarize to something you observe, you get locked into that which you polarize to. It is so important to remember—especially at times of great dramatic impact—that your safety lies within, that no solution that matters in the long run of things will be found outside of yourself. Your answers lie within.

CALM, GROUNDED, AND CENTERED
August 18, 2002

Well, now. The time of which we have spoken is close at hand. Before that occurs, we want to give you a last reminder—that this journey of yours is a PROCESS, not an event, and although you are reaching an important threshold, there is a journey to be made beyond that time, so please remember this and do not place yourself in a position of locked energy with regard to this "event."

We cannot emphasize too much that it is important to remain detached and to not get caught up in the drama that is unfolding all around you. The moment you engage with chaos, you get sucked into it. The moment you polarize to something you observe, you get locked into that which you polarize to. It is so important to remember—especially at times of great dramatic impact—that your safety lies within, that no solution that matters in the long run of things will be found outside of yourself. Your answers lie within. Even if you are not hearing "voices" or words, you do know—in each and every moment—what is true for you. You can access this knowing at any time. It is a feeling that you feel. Something will feel "right" or it will feel "off" or "wrong." Trust your feelings. Don't let anyone talk you out of them. It is not important that anyone else know what you feel. It is perfectly all right to keep your knowing to yourself, but don't let anyone sway you. There will be many attempts to talk you into adopting a certain attitude, but stay aligned with what you know as your own truth. You can carry it silently, but do not abandon it in order to accommodate anyone else.

We have been assessing things on your planet and we find two things are going on, neither of which come as a total surprise, given the "polarity game" and the lateness of the hour. First, the forces that use deception as their way of gaining polarity and taking energy from others have been succeeding in their plans for world domination. They are aided by those of higher densities of the same polarity and soon there will be an increase in their visibility. It is far too late to stop any of this, so we are just telling you this so you will understand what you see as it unfolds. They have succeeded so well, we must confess that it is rather humorous to us to see how easily they have made their way with so little resistance. However, we do know the "ending" of the story, and there does come a time when their "game" will be "up" and they will depart for another destination.

In the meantime, however, deception will be everywhere and on the increase from its present levels. That is why we emphasize that you go within for your "news." Everything is being manipulated to such an extent that nothing you read or hear is untouched, except possibly some of the material that comes through the clearest of channels. Those are few in number, and the greatest part of the channeled material that is available to you has been affected and corrupted until it is simply not true anymore. There will always be some noble sentiments sprinkled liberally about by all of these sources, but in the end, they are leading those who listen to them down a path that will only end in distrust and disappointment.

That being said, there are some events about to unfold that directly affect you and your world. We are here to support you and will have much more to say in the weeks ahead. There will be one more Message in this volume and then we will begin anew with Volume Three. The Messages are our gift to you and we hope that many more will find their way to reading them in the coming days, weeks and months. We are pleased to see how so many of you ARE taking our words seriously, and we note that the changes we have foretold are upon you. The "good news" is that the story has a happy ending. The "bad news" is that there are some relatively difficult days ahead for your planet and everything upon her. But that is not "news" to you at this point. We have been preparing you for a long time to receive the Grace that is available to you now. So many of you are "going with the flow" of change, and we are pleased that our words have in some way made that easier for you to do. You have been trained in the ways of surrender and your motto of "let go, let God" will serve you well in the times ahead.

The deceivers are massing now, and you will be hearing more from them of what they want you to hear and think. Each one will be claiming to have the "truth," the "inside story," and none of them will agree, but if you look behind the words, you will find the same background is there, no matter what "picture" is held up before your eyes. Do not be deceived. There are many predictions coming to a head in the next few months, and so many of them will fail to materialize. It is all part of how the deceivers get people to lose their trust in everything, so when the truth comes along, they throw that out, too. It is a way of getting people to give up all resistance to the coming tyranny, so they will more willingly play into the hands of those who are behind that scenario and scheme.

There is a children's story about a boy who got great fun out of warning the local people that a wolf was coming. It made him feel more powerful to see them scrambling about just because he convinced them that they were in danger. But when the wolf really DID come, the townspeople ignored him and they were all eaten alive. His false warnings caused them to mistrust him so totally that when there was a real danger to them, they ignored him and so they fell prey to the real wolf.

So you will be peppered with warnings about this danger and that danger and if you go running around as if they were something you could do anything about, you will find that nothing of what they say happens and then you will disregard the real warnings when they come. But if you tune into your inner voice and FEEL INTO THE VIBRATION, you will not be fooled. You will be able to tell when it "feels real," and whether you have to do anything at any given time. Many of you have already been feeling and responding to inner urges for change in your lives. Some of you have decided to move to a new place or leave an old relationship. Others are making many subtle changes in your perception and thinking and becoming clear of the chatter and noise of the world. The real changes are taking place within, where they are hidden. Because of the power of the physical senses, it is easy to be "outer directed" and to measure things by how they appear in the outer world. But your safety lies in being "inner directed" and by measuring with your subtle senses—how things FEEL to you, not how you "think" about them or what you hear from others, most especially the media.

We will not make predictions, other than to say that the time of the parting of the different destiny paths is nearly upon you. However, each of you has a plan for your life and each of you will have different experiences, so there is no prediction we can make that will be true for all of you, other than when the time is right, you will be called to your right place. Every detail of your life has been anticipated by your Oversoul. All of your "appointments with destiny" will be kept. Every last requirement will be met for the completion you are making with all of your other lives. You are already losing your memory capabilities and for some of you that is not convenient, but be encouraged by that sign that you are that much closer toward your desired destination. You are well along in your process and there is much Grace flowing. All you need to do is receive it.

Your inner knowing is your best armor against the deceptions. If something does not feel altogether true for you, TRUST that feeling. You must also trust in the plan for your life. You must trust that whatever you need to complete your life's purpose will be provided. That does not mean you will always like how it is wrapped, but every occurrence in your life is a true gift to help you complete your life in the way that was intended for you by your Oversoul. You exist as an extension of your Oversoul. You do not need techniques to activate or rearrange anything. Your life will bring you into perfect contact with the experiences needed for the fulfillment of your life's plan. Even those things that you might consider painful, unpleasant, or undesirable are still moving you toward the goal of completion. If unpleasant feelings arise, allow them to flow through you. Do not block them or repress them. That does not mean you have to act on them. Just allow them to flow through you.

A lot is being cleared at this time, and none of you is exempt from that. If you find yourself detaching more and more from the world around you, that is not a bad thing. That does not mean you are not a caring person. It just means you are becoming free from the influences of others as to how you should live your life. You can be your true self wherever you are. Just remember that you don't have to make a big noise about it. Just be it.

Things are beginning to intensify now and will continue to do so for the next few years, until all is complete. There has been a decision made to accelerate everything, which means that some of the things that we predicted would happen further out will now happen sooner. That means that BOTH kinds of things will be affected in this way—the things that you will be glad about and the other kind—the things that you might prefer didn't happen at all. For caring people like yourselves, it could get very difficult to avoid getting caught up in the coming drama, so detach. If you have to unplug the television set, do that. Put your time and energy into those things that nourish you, that bring you peace, and let your love flow. Polarization and resistance are two things that will greatly increase your discomfort, so we give you this simple exercise to do when you discover yourself getting caught up in the drama and chaos:

Wherever you are, whatever you are doing, just close your eyes and focus on your breath. Obviously, if you are driving a car or operating machinery, you don't want to do this until you have pulled off the road or stopped the machine, but even then, as soon as you can, disconnect from what "hooked" you and got you caught up in the drama. Close your eyes and focus on your breath. Deliberately take slow, deep breaths until you have regained a sense of your own self and are calm, grounded, and centered. Then very slowly open your eyes again and let yourself remain calm, grounded, and centered. Allow yourself to witness what is going on around you without getting caught up in it. If you find yourself getting "hooked" again, repeat the exercise. You may have to do this several times but do it. If you are in the midst of a heated conversation, do it. If the person insists on continuing the conversation while you have your eyes closed, hold up a finger or your hand, to indicate "Wait." This will help both of you. You will be setting an example that they can follow. "Wait."

You always have three choices: to do something, to not do something, or to wait for clarity before acting. Wait for clarity. There is very little in life that can't wait. If someone is bleeding to death in front of you, you wouldn't want to wait very long, but you must attain clarity more quickly in such circumstances. It is important to attain clarity before acting. Deepening your breathing is telling yourself that you are choosing calm over chaos. It is like a message to your body, "calm down." In the times ahead, it will be very important to remain calm, grounded, and centered.

There is nothing you can't handle if you remain rooted in the moment. We have spoken before about remaining rooted in the moment that is presenting, in what is also called the NOW. On Terra you will live in the NOW all of the time, so this is good practice for you.

A moment is a unit of experience. It has a beginning, a middle, and an end. You can feel when something begins to rise in energy in your life. It presents, then it swells to a climax, and then it recedes and resolves. That is a moment—from the time it arrives into your life until it recedes and resolves. Every moment arrives containing everything it needs for its completion. It unfolds perfectly, and even when you are in the midst of a challenging time, you can remain rooted in the moment and thus move through it with Grace. The more you can detach—the more you can ALLOW THE MOVEMENT—the more ease and comfort you will have in your journey through the days ahead. Resistance of any kind blocks the flow. You can remain rooted in your truth without resisting the flow that occurs all around you. Think of a tree with a stream flowing around it. The tree remains in place when it is rooted and grounded. Be that tree. This is not the same as stubbornness or resistance. Be rooted in the moment. Be rooted in your truth.

Keep your "inner ear" turned on and listening at all times. It helps to trust the flow of your life. If you feel overwhelmed by the speed of everything, just let it flow. Become still in the midst of the movement that is going on all around you. Let it flow. You are a great being, experiencing yourself as a little body. You are a great being who has helped create vast portions of the existing reality.

Breathe. Center. Ground. Bring calm to yourself as a choice. Choose calm. Choose peace. Choose serenity.

"The Coming Storm" is almost at your door. Let the winds rage all around you. Be peace in the midst of the storm. Do it for yourself and your loved ones. Be the gift that you are. You don't have to change anything. Be yourself. That's gift enough.

We leave you now, in peace and honor and blessing. Amen, Adonoy Sabayoth. We are the Hosts of Heaven.

NOTE: After receiving this Message, an astute reader mailed me a question about an apparent conflict in the material. She pointed out that in the first part of the Message, the Hosts found it almost humorous that the power elite's plans were met with so little resistance, and in the latter part of the Message, they encouraged us to not resist what was going on around us. I asked for a clarification, and this is what they gave me:

CLARIFICATION
August 24, 2002

A bit of clarification is in order, to clear up an apparent ambiguity in our most recent Message. As many of you may know, particularly astrologers, any particular quality or activity has the potential for a positive and a negative effect. For example, when you are considering the influences represented by a particular aspect in astrology, you can see the potentials for both a good quality and one that would not be considered good. Both can exist in the same aspect.

Just so with the concept of surrender. If you give up your resistance to a higher force in your life, the motives for your surrender must be considered in order to evaluate whether it is a positive thing or not, and the ultimate outcome is really what reveals the truth of it all. In the first example we gave, where we made note of the agenda of those with yearnings for global totalitarian power, we found it humorous to see how many people were willing to surrender their personal freedoms in return for some comfort and maintenance of their status quo. You COULD say that the same thing is true if one is being asked to give up resistance to the Creator's agenda, but in the first case, you are surrendering to the wills of other people, who want something from you that meets their needs, and in the second case, you are being asked to surrender your experience of separation from the Creator, so that your personal will comes into better alignment with the divine purpose for your life. From our perspective, there is a very big difference, both in the motives involved and the outcomes.

In surrendering to the Will of the Creator, you actually create greater freedom for yourself because then you simply have to follow the flow of your life, instead of remaining locked into the limited possibilities of what you can imagine while still in the veiled state of consciousness. You open up the portals for more to appear in your life that would have been considered miraculous or magical when measured in your formerly limited view. In the state of giving up resistance to the flow of your life, you are moving out of fear into a state of Grace. You are surrendering your need to control everything in order to keep your fear at bay. You are moving more into acceptance and trust in the plan for your life.

In surrendering your freedoms to those in control of your world in return for the appearance of security and retention of some portion of the material aspects of your life that give you comfort, you have made what is often referred to as a "devil's bargain." While you appear to gain something in the short term, when the time comes to "pay the bill," you then discover the true cost of what it is you have given up. If you look at that kind of non-resistance, you will find that it has fear at its base. So it is important to look at the motives that underlie a given action or decision. Are they based in fear or are they based in trust in the plan for one's life?

However, since all things are playing out according to the plan for each life, it is impossible to say that even a devil's bargain does not ultimately serve a higher purpose. We find it humorous to see the globalists achieving their goals so easily because we know the outcome of the whole drama. In the end, those who made that trade of freedom for material security and possessions will lose everything they bartered for, and even those who hold the reins of power now will be defeated. It strikes us as ironic that everything has a tendency to work out in opposite ways to how they appear in the beginning. Those who surrender their freedoms for material comfort will in the end lose both the freedoms AND the material comfort. Those who surrender their resistance to the divine plan for their life will ultimately "gain the kingdom," because they will be making the choices needed to come into their true inheritance, their true nature as the co-creators of this reality. In being willing to risk everything material, in the end they gain the ability to have and create anything material that they might desire, but from a state of total sovereignty rather than servitude.

We hope these remarks are helpful in clarifying any possible confusion created by our choice of words in the above Message, and we hope that they are also an impetus for you to reflect deeply on the choices that are presenting to you in each and every moment of your life. We are suggesting that you give your alignment with the Creator the highest priority. In one of your scriptures, it counsels you to "Seek first the kingdom. Then all else will be added." In bartering personal freedom for short-term material comfort, one ultimately loses everything that is precious in life and one has placed one's heart in the wrong place. This is not a new idea, but we ask you to contemplate the deeper possibilities of these two aspects of surrender. Whom or what do you surrender to and why?

We leave you now, in peace and honor, and blessing. Amen, Adonoy Sabayoth. We are the Hosts of Heaven.

... many things will be playing out on the planetary surface, and it is precisely for that reason that we will be silent for awhile. Those on the surface have to experience those times in certain ways, in keeping with the plan for their life, and they must do so unaided by us in order to have the fullest possible experience for themselves.

FAREWELL FOR AWHILE
September 15, 2002

We have asked to speak with you today because a threshold has been reached and it is now time to begin the Harvest. We will begin the Harvest with a relatively small group of you and then will return for still more. This will go on for the next few months until all of you who have not committed to staying on the ground will be lifted into another level and then some of you will come and go from that place for the time remaining until the Pole Shift. This "holding zone" is not a place on or inside of the planet, but another place, on another frequency band, where you can be worked with more directly and facilitated in the completion of your own transformation. Our beloved messenger will be included in this first group, but will be one of the ones who comes and goes until all is complete, so you do not need to be concerned about her availability.

The "Booster Rocket" event will occur later this year, but some of you will be lifted even before then. There is a scheduled time for each and every one of you, and when it comes your turn, you will know it with absolute clarity and certainty. You will not have to tell anyone anything, for if you need to inform anyone, we will give you that ability when the time comes. You see, there is no need to anticipate any of this. Just trust in the flow of your life and all will unfold perfectly, without harm to anyone. We have the ability to take people and return them to nearly the same moment in which they disappeared. When your transformation is complete, you will have the ability to change form to suit the circumstances, so if you need to look like you look at present, you will look like that. If it serves the greater good for you to look like something or someone else, you will look like that. You will all be very adapted to your circumstances, and as they flow and change, so you will also flow and change.

This communication will be the last one for Volume Two. There will be a hiatus in these Messages while this Harvest project proceeds, but Volume Three will be given when it is time for that. It will be different in content, tone, and information than these first two, and that is all we will say about that for now. So please do not be asking for the next Message. There will be a time of no Messages for awhile, as that is part of the Plan.

In the interim, many things will be playing out on the planetary surface, and it is precisely for that reason that we will be silent for awhile. Those on the surface have to experience those times in certain ways, in keeping with the plan for their life, and they must do so unaided by us in order to have the fullest possible experience for themselves. It would only diminish the intensity and richness of those times if we were there, commenting on every development. These two volumes will be available, for those who have "eyes to see" and "ears to hear." They will suffice to give the roadmap for those times. Then, when things have played out to a certain degree, we will again be heard from, in order to prepare people for the final stages of the drama and its conclusion. Our counsel to you would be to listen within at all times, during all activities in which you find yourself. Some animals have the ability to point their ears in different directions independently. We suggest you do the same. Point one ear outward, to receive the data from your environment, and point one ear inward, constantly listening to the whisperings of your intuition and "knowing." That inner voice is quiet and subtle most of the time. It is not like it is shouting at you. It is more gentle than that, so you must be able to hear it above the noise that surrounds you.

When your time comes, you will know it. Some of you know that you will be on the ground through the years ahead, because your particular part in the drama requires that. Do not feel either more or less special because of that. Everyone is totally equal in their importance with regard to the Plan. No voice will carry more weight than any other. No life is more or less important than any other. To think or feel otherwise is a matter of the separated self or ego. Some of you still are wrestling with your self-worth issues, and need to make these kinds of comparisons, but in the end, you are who you came to be, and the best thing is to be the best expression of that intention that you can. So now, all things will be coming to a head and moving toward the eventual conclusion. The acceleration is upon you already and will become even more intense as time passes and the tasks surface for completion. You might imagine a person with a clipboard, studiously marking off each "task" in a list of things that have to occur. Each thing must take place, and each thing WILL take place in its perfect time and sequence.

We feel a certain excitement in contemplating that this day has arrived. The measures have been taken and each one of you has been "fitted" with the necessary "equipment" to complete the rest of your journey through the remaining years of 3D Earth and beyond. All of the resources—both inner and outer—that you will require are now stored up and available to be used. A vast amount of preparation has gone into this effort, spanning thousands of years. You have experienced many lives in order to be perfectly equipped for this one and what now comes. It is truly a "grand finale," and great opportunity for the richness and complexity of all of the themes and threads that will be playing out from now on. Regardless of where your life leads you, we promise you one thing: it will not be boring! This is an incredible time to be in a body on planet Earth, and you will have much to reflect upon when it has all drawn to a close.

So in a sense, today we are saying "farewell for awhile." We promise you that we will be back when it is time for us to do so. For those of you who are moving on to complete your transformation, it will be a time when you find yourselves actually among us, face to face. For those who remain on the ground, you will be assisted directly by those who complete their transformation and come and go from that point on. They will appear in your midst at the needed times, and will disappear when that assistance is no longer needed. It will be impossible to know from day to day what to expect, as there will be many surprises on many fronts. We assure you that each and every person will have the experiences they are supposed to have, as chosen by their Oversoul. There are no accidents, and there are no real losses, only change. There is absolute certainty that each and every one of you will reach the destination chosen by your Oversoul, and will do so perfectly—in the right time, in the right way. None of you will be left alone, regardless of the form your assistance and support team takes. You will meet others like yourself, and you will gradually form small clusters of like-minded people. It will happen naturally. There is no need to create predesigned and preconceived communities. Follow the flow of your life, Remain rooted in the present. Deal fully with what presents to you in the moment. Remember that a moment is a unit of experience, not a unit of time. Live in the moment, moment by passing moment, and you will find yourself in exactly the right place at the right time.

In saying farewell for now, know that we are always with you, waking and sleeping, and we look forward to the time when you are ALL back with us once again.

Amen, Adonoy Sabayoth. We are the Hosts of Heaven.

NOTE: When I originally received this Message, I made the mistake of assuming the Hosts meant 2002 as "this year," when they referred to the Booster Rocket event as occurring "later this year." Apparently other people did, as well. The following article is an exploration of that issue and another test of faith that occurred around the same time. I have included it in this new edition as part of the ongoing story of Operation Terra. I hope it is helpful to you in your journey.

ON BEING PIONEERS

January 5, 2003

In the Messages, we are referred to as being pioneers. There is a great deal bound up in that simple word: "pioneers." It means many things, including the necessity of going through crises of faith—to reach deeper inside ourselves for inner resources we didn't know we had, to reach higher than ourselves, for help from the unseen. In their last Message, "Farewell For Awhile," the Hosts said they would be silent so that we could have the richest possible experience for ourselves. That Message was given on September 15, 2002, and in that same Message, they said that the "Booster Rocket" event would occur "later this year." I assumed, and I think all of us assumed, that they meant the Gregorian CALENDAR year of 2002. We assumed incorrectly, as I shall reveal below.

The Messages also stress the importance of facing down our fears. My greatest fear was that of being a "false prophet." I am a reluctant channel in the first place. The last thing I wanted to happen to me was to be given words to say that were not true. I have often been critical of other sources of channeled information because of the gross inaccuracies they put forth. As the end of the calendar year approached, I grew increasingly tense and anxious. What if nothing happened? What if the Booster Rocket event DID happen? The implied suffering was too terrible to contemplate, and I agonized over being "right" versus the deep wish that a peaceful outcome could be obtained. I watched in stunned amazement as the excuses for war grew thin at the same time as the preparations for war increased. What was going on?

Then, as the pressure mounted, I got a letter from someone in Canada, pointing out that one of the Messages ("Calm, Grounded, and Centered") was missing from the printed version of Volume Two. I take such pains to make sure the books are as perfect as I can make them before they go to the printer, so this was very discouraging news. I felt and still feel sick in my heart about this. I checked the file that I constructed the book from, and it was correct. How did this happen? And why? And what should I do about it?

I struggled with all of this in relative isolation. The only people who knew about it were my partner and a few of the people on the Forums, including a trusted friend of many years. I went through yet another "dark night of the soul," of which there have been so many. I went back and reviewed all of the demonstrations that I had been given about my path and the work I was to do. I believed with all my heart in the journey to Terra, the ships, and all the rest, and the Hosts had certainly been accurate about 9/11 before it had happened. And it was clear to me that world events WERE playing out toward a time that WOULD meet the conditions laid out for "Booster Rocket Time" (BRT), but it was also clear that it wasn't going to happen by the end of 2002. I assumed that I had been given false information, that I was seeing the realization of my worst fear—that I was, indeed, a "false prophet." And on top of that, with all the care and effort I had put into making the book perfect, it had a major flaw. An entire chapter was missing, and the "Clarification" of that Message ended up pasted onto the previous Message, where it made no sense whatsoever. I felt like my whole world was collapsing on top of my head, and it was not a happy time. And yet, when I woke up on New Year's Day, the birds were singing, it felt more like spring than winter, and I felt like the year would be a wonderful one, in spite of how it looked at the time.

There was another pioneer in the first half of the last century. His name was Aurobindo, and he and his spiritual partner, a woman referred to only as "Mother," dedicated their lives to the search for the key to the next phase in human evolution. Aurobindo made the observation that when it is time for an evolutionary leap, there is a pressure that builds up and then a leap occurs relatively suddenly. He compared it to putting pressure on one end of a melon seed, and when the pressure was great enough, the seed would leap across space and land far from its original position. These past two weeks for me were just such a pressure. I let go and let God, over and over again. The final blow however, came yesterday, when the first letters came in, questioning the authenticity and accuracy of the Messages, and some people began leaving the mailing list and the Forums. I was in despair and confusion as to what I should do. I absolutely would not try to explain or defend myself. If this is what God wanted for my life, so be it!

I understood what Christ must have felt in the Garden of Gethsemane when the pressure was on him. I understood how Buddha must have felt when he was confronted by the many tests of his faith. I understood how the path of initiation into higher states of consciousness seems to include these tests of faith, to require us to venture out into uncharted territory with no guidebook or map to show us the way. That is what a pioneer is called upon to do, by definition. We are pioneers, according to what the Messages say, so these crises of faith are part of the journey to Terra, as well as being part of the path of initiation into a higher state of consciousness.

Last night, the pressure was so great that I was determined to get an answer from the Hosts before I would go to bed. This is what they said, as I wrote down their words on a pad of paper:

All right now. We have several points to make:

1) We have not misled you. We have not told you anything that is not true. We have not led you to make a "failed prediction."
2) We are still with you. We are guiding every step you take. You are on the right course.
3) Booster Rocket Time is upon you NOW. The passage of a few days more and all will be fulfilled.
4) You are still in charge of the "op" and much more lies ahead to be done.

Having said all of this, we do understand your position and shall give you this assurance: All WILL be well, and this pain will soon pass. Have faith. The best is yet ahead. You will always have critics, regardless of what does or does not happen. But we WILL see you through.

Q. Did YOU tell me about "by the end of this year"?

A. Yes, but we did not mean the calendar year. We meant the year end when the spring comes and begins the new cycle.

Amen, Adonoy Sabayoth. We are the Hosts of Heaven."

When I reflected on this, I realized that this definition of the year made a great deal of sense, as it is a celestial point of reference and transcends all individual cultures. It is a true reflection of the planet's rotation around the sun, and the major monuments at Stonehenge, in Central America, and in Egypt all are aligned in relation to this cycle, not the Gregorian or Chinese or Hebrew or Mayan or Moslem calendars. According to a Web site located at http://www.celebratetoday.com/newyears.html, it's possible to identify a new year in every month of the calendar. One can celebrate Sekhmet in January, Chinese New Year in January or February, Noruz in March, Baisakhi in April, Buddhist New Year in May, Runic New Year in June, Armenian New Year in July, Shenshai New Year in August, Rosh Hashanah in September, Samhain in October, Dipavali in November, and Papal States New Year in December.

The calendar defined by the solstices and equinoxes underlies the dictionary definition of a year, namely "the period of time during which the Earth completes a single revolution around the sun." The Hosts speak to us all, regardless of nationality, religion, or geographic location, and it is obvious that the time one chooses to begin and end a year is both arbitrary and subjective. The "vernal" equinox (northern hemisphere) on March 20 marks the beginning of the celestial year in Western astrology, but Chinese astrology would not use that point of reference. In the southern hemisphere, the seasons are reversed, but I live in the northern hemisphere and since I interpret the telepathic impress through my own symbol system (that's how telepathy works), I translate it "spring," whereas someone in the southern hemisphere might call it "autumn." It's all subjective, and the Hosts have now defined their "year" as ending on March 20, 2003.

My partner has suggested that this all happened for a reason. He suggests that the reason is so that all of us who made the assumption that the Hosts meant the Gregorian CALENDAR year can be shaken out of our narrow cultural frame of reference into a planetary perspective, which in my thinking brings us back to some of the fundamental principles involved with Operation Terra: We are here for the planet, and we come from every race and culture, background and religion. We are in the East. We are in the West. This crisis of faith in the Hosts' words paradoxically put us squarely back on ourselves, to re-examine the basis of our beliefs and what we align with. In the end, we have to let go and let God.

My partner suggested that the missing chapter in the book was so that the book would have to be reprinted and that this lesson in faith would become part of that book also. I really don't presume to have all of the answers, or even many of them. I am just like everyone else on this journey. I am doing the best I can to understand what "God wants for my life," and if I get too filled with self-importance and feeling too special, I am humbled so I can remember that it is not about me or being right, it is about "getting right with God." It is about right alignment, about the walk and tasks of being a pioneer, about being willing to go into uncharted territory and to let go and let God show us the way. To do that with faith and trust is the "mission."

It is ironic that the Message that disappeared from the book was one that directs us to listen within ourselves for what is true for us alone, in every moment. More specifically, that Message had told us, "...we want to give you a last reminder—that this journey of yours is a PROCESS, not an event, and although you are reaching an important threshold, there is a journey to be made beyond that time, so please remember this and do not place yourself in a position of locked energy with regard to this 'event.'" They went on to add, that "no solution that matters in the long run of things will be found outside of yourself. Your answers lie within. Even if you are not hearing "voices" or words, you do know—in each and every moment—what is true for you. You can access this knowing at any time. It is a feeling that you feel. ... There will be many attempts to talk you into adopting a certain attitude, but stay aligned with what you know as your own truth. You can carry it silently, but do not abandon it in order to accommodate anyone else." And finally, they said, "each of you has a plan for your life and each of you will have different experiences, so there is no prediction we can make that will be true for all of you, other than when the time is right, you will be called to your right place." In other words, regardless of the source of the information, the answers lie within, and at a certain point, the only thing that is prudent to do is to follow your own inner promptings in each moment and "let go, let God" with everything else.

I hope this is helpful in some way to you. I yearn more than ever for the peace, joy and love of Terra, but I am still willing to walk the walk that is asked of me, today and every day, until it is over. I hope that you will do the same.

Peace and love,
Lyara

AUTHOR'S NOTE, November 2004: In hindsight, it is clear that the US offensive dubbed "Shock and Awe" did indeed occur on March 20, 2003, precisely within the timeframe the Hosts had defined. The buildup to it had been long and tedious, and it did not appear to be quite the "shock" that we expected would occur. However, there can be no doubt that it was a defining moment in world history and the aftermath has revealed a world that is much changed and will never be the same.

I find it interesting that the very first weapons launched in that offensive were Tomahawk missiles, and they had booster rockets attached to them to enable them to clear the decks of the ships from which they were being launched before their own propulsion system kicked in to carry them to their targets. There was no way I could have anticipated that little detail when I received the Message "Booster Rocket Time," and once again the Hosts have shown us that our understanding is not the same as theirs is — they have amazed me over and over with the precision and relevance of their words, which becomes even more clear with the passage of time.

SUPPLEMENTARY MATERIAL

(What follows is the original vision that I received in 1982 and which depicts the events that are playing out now. It was the blueprint of all that has developed since then, and I share it with you so that you can know what it is that I saw and experienced.)

A VISION OF THINGS TO COME
March, 1982

Then my teacher said, "Ask them [my guides] to show you what there is to see."

I said out loud, "Show me what there is to see." On my "mental screen" [eyes closed], I saw what looked like a movie screen roll down. First the screen was blank. Next to it, I saw a Chinese gentleman. He had long mustaches and was wearing a long robe. He unrolled a long scroll, which was a checklist of the "duties" that had to be performed [i.e. the things that had to happen]. As he began to consult the scroll, my attention was drawn to the screen, where I saw a globe shape take form. As I drew closer to the globe, I knew that I was looking at the Earth.

I saw a grey, pointed mountain with a green slope in front of it. The mountain blew up (erupted) and opened a rift down its side that spread forward, opening a crevasse in the ground in front of it. Then I saw a full moon over the ocean. The wind began blowing very hard, whipping up foam and huge waves on the oceans. [Note: the scenes "dissolved" into one another, and I was only conscious of what I was seeing, and of describing it to my teacher, who made notes as I talked.] Tall trees were being blown over. I saw people running, frightened, screaming. Large cities toppled over, tall buildings just giving way. The sky behind was red from the burning — everything was burning. I saw what looked like a man holding his child and struggling up a steep slope, trying to escape, but sliding back down each time. There was no escape. All was confusion, greyness ... there was a tremendous amount of confusion...

(As I peered into all this confusion, suddenly I understood: "There's not enough love, [teacher]! There's not enough love!)

In the midst of the confusion, with all the people in grey running about, here and there people clothed in white robes began appearing. This was happening all over the world. Wherever they appeared, centers of calm occurred in the confusion. They began appearing in greater and greater numbers now, like popcorn when it begins to pop. They were calm in the midst of the confusion, giving blessing, their presence soothing and calming those around them. (The phrase came in, "They are centers for calm and blessing.") Order began taking form out of the chaos; the ones in white began to form columns, like wave forms — herding, gathering the ones in grey, calming them into steadily moving groups, herding them into an orderly procession, climbing up into the openings of vast hovering vehicles. It was a massive, world-wide exodus ... a tremendous undertaking ....

I drew back into space, where I beheld the Earth hanging in the sky. The Earth slowed, then stopped rotating, throwing off the water from its surface in great white clouds. It hung motionless for a moment, and then it rolled over slowly, like a top falling over that has lost momentum. Then the Earth began spinning on a different axis ...

(There was a discontinuity in the vision at this point. Most of the people who had been taken off the Earth were carried to other parts of the solar system and Universe to complete their lives. After the Earth had time to heal, about 10% of the people were brought back to what looked like a large planet, to be equipped for their return to Earth. This included reprogramming of their consciousness, as well as equipping them with clothing, supplies, and technology. None of the "old" pattern was to be reintroduced to the "New Earth.")

The "New Earth" is polished, gleaming, like mother-of-pearl. There is great gleaming light everywhere. It is now reinhabited. The sky is incredibly blue. I hear this beautiful music, which I know is the "music of the spheres." The plants are bright and joyous; they exult in the shining light and the clean air. The people move in quiet joy, radiantly being there. Everyone and everything is completely, blissfully conscious of their direct connectedness to the Creator.

Now I see Jesus on His throne ... incredible love streaming forth ... how much there is ... we don't have to be limited ... He will be with me throughout all this ... I am surrounded by his Love, his blue-white light... I feel so small ... "only if ye be as a little child."... I am totally enfolded in His Love.

I could not speak for some time afterward, so strong had been that experience of being totally enfolded in Jesus' love.

(The thoughts come)... Meanwhile, be in a prayerful attitude, feeling gladly serving. Attitude is the most important thing; the nature of the activity doesn't matter. Be in an attitude of readiness ... I'll be called ... Be ready when the call comes ... incredible amount of Love ... cherishing... .

Many years of training and preparation followed, culminating in the creation of Operation Terra and the receiving of the Messages. At this point in time, my role with regard to Operation Terra will change from that of a messenger to that of a teacher and support person for those who are on the ground during the "days ahead." Ours is a mission to create haven for those who are heading to Terra and will be gathered together over the few years that remain before the final cataclysms, evacuation, and Pole Shift ring down the curtain on the entire drama, once and for all.

If you want to be kept informed as things proceed, contact information is on page 158 of this book. Good journey!

YOU DON'T HAVE TO DIE

When a caterpillar hatches out of its egg and begins to eat leaves, it has certain characteristics in common with all other caterpillars. Its body is made up of many segments, each with a pair of legs, so it also has many legs. Its mouth is designed to chew on leaves, its eyes are simple, and it does not have antennae on its head.

It has a soft body, covered with a flexible skin, and it must crawl in order to get around. The caterpillar placidly munches its way through its growth phase, crawling around from one leaf to another. Then one day, an internal timing mechanism goes off, orchestrated by its glands and hormones, and the caterpillar spins a chrysalis around itself until it is completely enclosed. The chrysalis hardens and then a most miraculous transformation occurs.

Tucked safely inside its chrysalis, the caterpillar's body dissolves almost entirely (histolysis). Only the heart still beats. The rest is a gooey "soup" of organic materials with no form at all. If we were to open the cocoon at that point, the "goo" would never become anything. It would just die. However, if it is not harmed or interrupted, the "goo" forms up into another shape altogether—that of the developing butterfly. Instead of a soft skin, it forms a hard shell. Instead of a mouth that is adapted to chew leaves, it develops a long tube, curled into a tightly wound spiral, designed to reach deep into flowers and suck out their nectar.

The eyes form as part of the head, and are complex. Instead of many segments, there are only three, each with a pair of legs. And instead of being confined to crawling in order to get around, a delicate and intricate system of membranes, framework, and muscles takes shape; it will become the butterfly's wings. All of this takes place in secret, hidden away from the eyes of potential predators, but it is truly one of the miracles of nature.

Finally, all is complete. The butterfly emerges from the chrysalis and perches on a leaf or stalk, but its wings are tiny and crumpled from being folded tightly against its body. Then its heart pumps fluid into the wings and they expand. The wings gradually unfold to their

143

final size and shape. Finally the framework hardens as they dry in the air. Then the butterfly takes flight, a totally different creature than the caterpillar it used to be.

What, then, has happened to the caterpillar? Has it died? No, of course not. It has simply changed form.

When we speak of people dying, we mean the process in which the spirit separates from the body, leaving it behind to decay into its more elemental components, while the spirit moves on to occupy another plane of reality. We have all done this so many times that it is easy to forget that it is not always necessary to do this when it is time to move on to another phase of our existence. Just as the caterpillar has not "died" (i.e. left its body behind) in order to become a butterfly, we do not have to die (i.e. leave our bodies behind) in order to become our "new selves" for the new Earth, Terra. We simply have to change form.

When various spiritual writings make reference to a "glori-fied body," it is this new kind of form that is being referred to. In order to understand this, one needs to consider the spectrum of existence. We each occupy a spectrum of reality that spans from these dense physical bodies up through many levels—each one of a finer substance than the one below it—to a level where we are pure consciousness and light. If you pass white light through a prism, it will spread out into bands of different colored light. A rainbow exhibits these colors when sunlight passes through a mist of water droplets, each of which acts as a tiny prism that splits the light into those bands of color with which we are so familiar.

When the pure Light of the Creator is spread into different bands of reality—different "planes" or "dimensions"—it vibrates at different frequencies, just as the different colors of light vibrate at different frequencies. At the level of 3D physical matter, with our physical eyes, we can generally see colors from red (the lowest/ slowest frequency we can perceive) through violet (the highest/ fastest frequency we can perceive). But there is also light below the frequency that we can perceive (infrared, for example) and light above the frequency we can perceive (ultraviolet, for example) with our physical eyes. It is THERE, but we cannot perceive it because our instruments of perception (in this case, our eyes) are limited to a certain range of frequencies.

In the transformation we will make on our way to Terra, we will be shifting our own frequency and we will then be able to perceive a different range of frequencies than are available to us now. Terra already exists—right here, right now—but we cannot perceive her (except with clairvoyant vision) because we have not shifted into the same frequency band that she occupies. In order to see and experience her directly, we have to make a shift in consciousness, frequency, and perception. They are inextricably linked.

Each different "plane" or frequency band within the reality spectrum vibrates across a discrete range of frequencies. Each "form" that we occupy takes its characteristics from the frequency band it occupies. We have different bodies for each part of the spectrum of reality. The bodies we are in right now are the appropriate vehicles for us at this level of reality, just as the caterpillar's body was uniquely adapted to its type of existence as a crawling insect. However, in order to inhabit Terra, we have to become "butterflies"—we have to transform into totally different kinds of bodies that will be the appropriate vehicles for that level of reality.

When the Messages say that we do not have to die, it is the same as the caterpillar-to-butterfly transformation: there is just a change in form, but the particular lifestream continues without interruption. Those of us who are destined to colonize Terra will not die; we will simply change form. In fact, we are already well on our way to doing just that.

There are those who will incarnate on Terra through the birth process, just as babies incarnate through the birth process here on Earth. But where will the sperm and eggs and wombs to create and nurture those babies come from? Some adult forms must be provided in order to "seed" and colonize the new planet. They must come from somewhere. That is part of what Operation Terra is about: gathering up the seed stock for the new world. This process is referred to as the Harvest. When wheat ripens, it provides the seeds that will become the next crop.

Some of us are destined to be the progenitors of a whole new species of beings, and in order to do that, we ourselves must transform our bodies into those that are appropriate for the new world.

That is why it is said that we do not have to die: we are taking our bodies with us. It should be noted that the Heaven's Gate group did *not* take their bodies with them. Therefore, if they did indeed end up at "the next level above human," as they claimed they would, they did so only as spirits. In other words, they "died." They will have to wait for other adults to conceive the fetuses into which they can enter, in order to experience physical existence at that level of reality, if it is their destiny to do so.

You may point out that in the caterpillar-to-butterfly example, the caterpillar may just change form, but the butterfly eventually completes its life cycle, lays the eggs for the new generation of caterpillars, and then "dies" (leaves its body behind). That is true for 3D butterflies, but when we have completely transformed our consciousness to that of our next level of being, we will complete each life after that by consciously choosing to change form, again and again and again. We will never again have to leave our body behind (which is what is meant by dying), so therefore, we will never have to "die" again.

This transformation is going to happen to a fairly large number of people—several million, in fact—so it has to be a well-established process in order for it to happen to so many in the relatively short time left for 3D Earth to shift into 4D. We are indeed the "last generation" spoken of in the scriptures, regardless of our chronological age. There are not many years left before Earth will "graduate" At some point, Operation Terra will gather up those who will be the pioneers in the new world. Blessings to you on your way.

QUESTIONS AND ANSWERS
February 8, 2000

Q: *How do we accomplish the change from this body to the next?*
A. Operation Terra is a cooperative venture. Those of us who have volunteered to incarnate and act as the "ground crew" are being assisted by many more of their brothers and sisters in the higher realms. *They* are the ones who are overseeing your transformation. It is a known process and they are fully versed in the mechanics. You have actually been moving in this direction for several years, but now you are in the "final approach"—the onramp to the next world.

The first wave is in the process of being transformed now. The third wave will not undergo this process until after they are lifted. The second wave will undergo this process at a later time, depending on their "job assignment." The process requires a purification of all the cellular memory, both of the particular body and race consciousness, and the individual personality's accumulation of karmic debris. It also requires the linking up—atom for atom, molecule for molecule—of the present body's structure with the future analog or template of the body into which it will transform. For the first wave, the purification is not usually complete, so when this linkup occurs, there is some dissonance between the present body and the future analog, and this can cause some physical discomfort and low energy levels. However, this phase only lasts 2 to 3 weeks, so the discomfort is minimal in terms of the longer process.

Once the linkup and the purification are complete, there is a sort of "roll-up" that occurs. The present body traverses an energetic membrane and is subsumed into the new body. It will feel a little like a glove being turned inside out. One can have a similar feeling doing a somersault. There is a feeling of rolling over or rolling into as one releases oneself into the new form. For those who are ready, the moment will present itself very clearly, and there will be a certain act of faith required in accepting the full consequences of completing the action. Once the change has occurred, it is essentially irreversible, and in choosing to make the change, one is leaving behind all ties to the former identity and life. For the first wave, this will not be as difficult as for the ones who come later, as they have already undergone a profound stripping away of their former identity, so little is left to "leave behind." All is in Divine order, being orchestrated by each Oversoul, so one need not worry about the details. It is what you have been waiting for, for a very long time.

Q. *What is the time frame for all of this?*

A. We cannot give you a specific date or time frame, as that would infringe on your free will choices. However, we can say that the first wave is already past the "point of no return," similar to the point at which the fetus is in the birth canal and there is no more turning around. One simply endures the process for as long as it takes and then one emerges into a wholly new reality. We are overseeing each and every one of you and are trying to minimize the discomfort you may experience. Each one of you is being personally tended by a team of beings who are dedicated to your successful transformation. For those who will transform in the second and third waves, your experience will be somewhat different. Those in the second wave will be directly assisted by those of the first wave who have completed their transformation, and may be lifted off the planet if required to be provided with a protected environment in which to complete the change. The second wave will be needed to receive and help those of the third wave, who will be lifted off the planet and make their change while the planet herself is completing her own transformation. It is an "event" that is progressing in stages. We can also say that there is an outer threshold by which it must all complete, for there are cosmic cycles and rhythms involved that are not subject to alteration. Earth has a date with destiny and HER schedule drives everything else about our efforts to harvest the seed stock to colonize the new world.

Q. *What will we look like after this transformation?*

A. You will still look "human," but your form will be that of the true Adamic seed. Your present form is the result of the genetic manipulation by the interlopers, and you share in characteristics of simians (apes) and certain negative-polarity ETs. Your scientists have long wondered where the human pubic and axillary (armpit) hair patterns have come from. None of the other mammals have them. They are the expression of the genes from the negative-polarity ETs. The true Adamic model has hair on the scalp, eyebrows, and eyelashes, but nowhere else. The areola—that area of bald skin around the nipples—is the mammalian pattern from the simian genes. That also is not part of the Adamic model. You will have small nipples, but no areolas.

Your bodies will be perfect in every way. Every individual will be like what you might call a "god" or "goddess." Your bodies will be somewhat luminous and iridescent, but otherwise appear quite solid to you. Your form will be somewhat under your conscious control, and eye color may change to reflect your mood. There was a fad in the '60s for "mood rings" that were supposed to change color based on your mood. They worked on the principle that a change in mood produced a different skin temperature, and the material in the rings changed color with small changes in skin temperature. In your new bodies, your emotional "moods" will affect your eye color in a similar way. The more intense moods will produce different colors than the more relaxed ones. Not only will there be no privacy in thoughts (everything is consciously connected with everything else and "knows" everything in every moment, in every interaction), you will not be able to hide your emotional state from one another. No more secrets! This might be a breath of fresh air in some ways, but it will take some getting used to!

As you can see, there is much more we can say about this future of yours, but it is time to close for now. More information will be forthcoming. We leave you in peace and honor and blessing. Amen, Adonoy Sabayoth. We are the Hosts of Heaven.

MY/OUR STORY

In the beginning, we were just vast regions of consciousness, containing within us entire universes, spangled with galaxies and stars and planets—the stuff of creation. We are creator-gods, individualized portions of the One Infinite Creator, who are assigned the job of spinning off different realities in which the Infinite One can play. In this particular instance, 144,000 of us came together to form the reality in which you have established your present focus of awareness. We were each a particular "slant" or "angle" of the One Light, something like the little pieces of glass on a disco ball, reflecting the light in a slightly different way and sparkling at different times as the whole ball rotates through the beam.

So it has been, throughout the billions of years of our partnership. We precipitated this reality out of our joined fields of being and made a pact to be responsible for our creation. Some of us have elected to project portions of ourselves into our creation and to participate in it at various times, wearing different "costumes" for our various roles upon the stage of creative play. We have been both humble denizens of the most obscure realities and the luminaries that lit the way and redirected the course of "history" when it strayed from the original plan. We have come in all ages, and in all cultures worldwide. Our story is a collective story, for though we have appeared in the clothing of flesh, we never lost our identity as members of one family, the Hosts of Heaven. If you have been drawn to read these words, then this may be your story, also. You are probably one of us and soon you shall be reunited with your true family, your brothers and sisters in the many mansion worlds of the One Infinite Creator. When we have completed our task of seeing this planet through this transition into becoming Terra, our "mission" will be complete, and others shall come to pick up the task of carrying on. We will separate and go on to other forms of service to the Creator, and play in other fields of creation.

We each came to do a particular job, play a particular role, and now the dance is nearly over. We will all be leaving soon, and I am given the task of pointing the way for others to follow.

150

I remember standing together in a group—the ones I call the "tall beings." I have seen them several times, and I know them to be the ones with whom I am most closely connected. We planned who among us would come in, when and how we would connect up with each other, and who would do what. We planned who we would be born to and what portion of the Earth's sorrows we would take on to transform within ourselves. We created ourselves with all the capabilities and proclivities that we would need to complete our task, and we made agreements to help one another when that would become necessary in the course of our lives. Ours was to be a lonely passage, as our greatest strengths would only be honed in the isolation from others of our kind. Even now, most of us are hidden from one another, except for those few who have an intimate role in assisting us toward our completion with this plane.

I remember screaming all the way in, as I plummeted down from the vastness of my beingness and the wrappings made me smaller and smaller and smaller. I had made the agreement to do this, but the actual journey into this plane was a shock, the first of so many to follow. We have all had to endure so many traumas, from very early in life, but now we can leave that behind. It is time for use to reunite with our true family, our brothers and sisters here on Earth and in the higher dimensions around us.

Each of us plays a part in so many other lives. Each of us appears on the stage of another's drama at the perfect moment to supply our part in that individual's scenario, and we reciprocally receive from them that portion of our own. We are all part of one Body, and we reciprocally support one another's journey in a way that is totally perfect, when seen through a large enough lens.

I will just sum up my early years by saying that when I reached age 8, I realized that there was nowhere for me to express my true nature—not at home, not at school, not within my larger family. I remember acknowledging that "something in me knows where I am going" and I consciously chose to "leave," with the intention of coming back when I was out on my own in the world. However, when I did try to "come back" after I left college and was indeed out on my own, I couldn't find where I had gone, so I spent the rest of my years trying to find my way back to myself.

The breakthrough came in early 1981, when an unexpected event changed the course of my life forever. My life at that time was made up of my Amway business, a quiet home life with my husband (he worked for the State), and our life in the Jewish community. Every month, our Amway sponsor (an older woman who was sort of a second mother to her flock of distributors) held a potluck. One couple (charismatic Catholics) always said the grace and went around saying things like "Lord Jesus loves you" in almost every sentence. As a practicing Jew, this initially made me very uncomfortable, but eventually my curiosity overcame my discomfort and I decided to read the New Testament for the first time. I tried reading the King James Version, but there were passages that didn't feel had been translated correctly, so I asked one of my Amway customers to recommend another version. I went to the library to look for a copy, but they only had a pocket edition of the Revised Standard Version, so I took that one home instead. Next to it on the shelf was a copy of *In Search of Historic Jesus*, which I also checked out. I put both books on my nightstand, because it is my habit to do my reading at night, before I fall asleep.

The books were both there when a strange weakness overcame me two days later. I could barely get out of bed to go to the bathroom or to the kitchen for a little food. I was not sick or running a fever, but I didn't seem to have the strength to do anything, so I read. I read *In Search of Historic Jesus* first. It all seemed so oddly familiar, but I didn't know why at the time. When I got to the part that described what it was like to die by crucifixion, I was overwhelmed with sadness and grief about the suffering this man had gone through. It all seemed to be hitting so close to home, yet there was no explanation for the intensity of my feelings. I then read the four gospels, and again it seemed oddly familiar, but there didn't seem to be any reason why it should be so.

I had never doubted my identity as a Jew and never felt a need to go beyond the traditions I had been raised with. I was puzzled by my feelings of familiarity towards the accounts in the New Testament and the other book, so I turned to read Isaiah next. I had heard that Isaiah had prophesied the coming of Christ, and wanted to see whether it was true or not. I had never really read the Old Testament, either, as I was content with the Bible stories I had been taught in Sunday school while I was growing up, and knew enough to follow the services at Temple without further study on my part. As I read Isaiah and came to the part about a "young woman shall conceive" and bear a son whose name would be Immanuel, it was obvious to me from the context that that passage was not about Christ, but had been about something that would occur during Isaiah's lifetime. However, when I got to Isaiah 52-54, the account of the "suffering servant" leapt off the page at me as a description of the life I had just read about in the New Testament and *In Search of Historic Jesus*. I was stunned. How could this be? It seemed so clear to me that Isaiah had indeed prophesied the coming of Christ and the suffering he would go through, but why had I been raised to deny all of it as having happened?

I turned off the light and lay there in the darkness, my mind whirling and my thoughts bouncing back and forth between what I had been raised with and what seemed so apparent to me in what I had just read. I struggled to resolve the apparent conflict, to no avail. Finally, in frustration, I flung out a thought into the darkness (I didn't want to wake my sleeping husband): "If you (meaning Christ) are there, please let me know in a way that I can know!"

The thought seemed to hang in the air for a moment, and then it took on form. I "felt" someone materialize in our bedroom, and I "knew" it was "he" whom I had addressed. He moved silently from the foot of the bed where he had appeared and came to stand behind my head (never mind that there was a wall there!). Then he put his hands on my head and they were as real and solid as any I have ever felt. He put his knowledge and power into me and a brilliant cone of light shot out from my solar plexus. Suddenly, without hearing a word, I "knew" several things (keep in mind that I was totally unschooled in Christian doctrine). I "knew":

1. that I had lived my life in ignorance up to that point, and I was forgiven for all my errors, but from that moment forth I would be held accountable for my every thought, word, and deed;

2. that I was being called to a narrow path, and that if I deviated even so much as a millimeter from that path, I would only harm myself. I could never harm anyone except myself;
3. that there is no sin, only error, and that if we don't "get it right," we will get to do it over and over until we do "get it right."

I had absolutely no context for understanding this, but I could not deny the reality of the experience. Thus began my journey of stumbling back toward the Light. I wish I could say I went gracefully, but I didn't. Every lesson was won through the wearing down of my very considerable degree of resistance. I often joke that I was "bashed into surrender," and that I went down my path "kicking, and hollering, and screaming" all the way. But graceful or not, I have stayed the course that was put before me that night (March 9, 1981). In 1982, I received the vision (see page 124) that charted the course that my life is about—the journey to Terra.

It was not easy. It demanded everything of me that I had, and much that I did not know I had in me. I had to choose—over and over—to reach higher and deeper. It was agonizing, and there were so few to share the journey with. In 1984, I had a total breakdown of my immune system and it took 9 years of being a "bubble person" to work my way back to being functional again. During that time and afterward, I had the opportunity to explore the themes of sexual and verbal abuse, codependency, abandonment, and betrayal by those closest to me. I learned to distinguish between those things and people that supported and nourished life and those that did not. I learned about UFOs, ETs and angels, and I learned to channel. I "remembered" other lives, including one I had lived as a member of Christ's inner circle. I learned that my most important lives in terms of influencing the course of world history came before some of my most insignificant lives, destroying the theory that we live our lives in some sort of linear progression from "lowest" to "highest." I had many mystical experiences about the nature of God and the nature of reality, all of which I subsequently found had a scientific basis in holographic theory and quantum physics.

I was in a class of one in a solitary classroom, being lovingly but firmly taught by my mentors in unseen realms. My personal "team" included "Christ" (Jesus/Sananda), Archangel Michael, beings from other star systems, Babaji, and my soul family, the Hosts of Heaven. I lost everything I had in the material world—twice! I was taken further and further away from everything I knew and took my identity from until now it is nearly gone. It is very similar to the process I saw my mother go through as she left this world and her body, except I will not die a physical death. Mine is the "death" of my ego-identification. I will go on to another level and do my part to create the bridge to the new earth, Terra. Christ has been with me every step of the way, along with his "crew" of angels and ETs, and I have no doubt that he will see me through whatever steps remain in that journey.

It is far more peaceful for me now. My shell has been broken open and I am no longer trying to "keep it together." It is so much easier now to just let go and melt. Seeing my mother across from this life to the other side opened my heart in a way that has left me in a far more loving and accepting place. I used to be caught up in the ideas of "good and evil," but now I know it is all just God, wearing Its many costumes. I see how those I have labeled as evil are simply in a great deal of pain and have disconnected themselves from others so that they can project their pain onto them rather than feel it themselves. I feel I am nearly complete with my journey through 3D, with all of its lessons and teachings. In the end, it always has been about love. It is still about love.

I was told in my vision of 1982 that I would be "called." I believe that calling began when I was asked to deliver the messages from the Hosts of Heaven. I will continue to write as things come forward to be written, but if there comes a time when there are no more words to say, let this be my legacy to you. As the fox told the Little Prince, "It is only with the heart that one can see rightly; what is essential is invisible to the eye."

Each of you that is reading this article has your own version of this story. You have had your own themes to explore, but when it was time, you were also led through the steps of your awakening, just as I have been. Now you are here, reading these words. If they ring true to you, you have found a point of connection with your destiny path. I hope that these words will lead you to recognize the perfection of your own enfolding path, and the comfort that comes with knowing there is not much further to go.

I leave you now in peace and honor and blessing. Amen, Adonoy Sabayoth. We are (all of us) the Hosts of Heaven.

SUGGESTED READING

P.M.H. Atwater, *Future Memory* (especially pages 84 and 86).
Hampton Roads Publishing Company, Inc., 1999

Itzhak Bentov, *Stalking the Wild Pendulum: On the Mechanics of Consciousness*, reprint edition. Inner Traditions Ltd. 1988

David Bohm, *Wholeness and the Implicate Order*, reissue edition. Routledge, 1996.

George M. Lamsa, *Holy Bible: From the Ancient Eastern Text, George M. Lamsa's Translation from the Aramaic of the Peshitta*. Harper San Francisco, 1985.

Jose Stevens, Ph.D., *Transforming Your Dragons: Turning Personality Fear Patterns Into Personal Power*. Bear & Co, 1994.

Michael Talbot, *The Holographic Universe*, reprint edition. Harperperennial Library, 1992.

Gary Zukav, *The Dancing Wu Li Masters: An Overview of the New Physics*, reissue edition. Bantam Books, 1994.

ABOUT THE AUTHOR

Sara Lyara Estes, known as "Lyara" on the Web, earned a B.S. in Zoology (cum laude) from the University of Michigan, a Lifetime Teaching Credential (K–9) from California State University, and an MBA in Information Systems from Golden Gate University. She also held real estate and securities broker's licenses, had 1200 hours of training in energy systems and bodywork at the New Mexico Academy of Advanced Healing Arts, and received formal training in accessing other planes of reality from several teachers — those in bodies upon the planet and those in the planes above it.

In her work in medical research laboratories, Sara developed the first reliable method for cloning tissue and identified a previously unknown cell type that proved significant in immunology related to organ transplants. She served as a key research *subject* in the original biofeedback experiments conducted by Dr. Joe Kamiya at Langley-Porter Neuropsychiatric Institute and was also tested for her telepathic abilities in his laboratory, with a success rate of 100%. Walter Cronkite featured her in a *21st Century* TV segment, "Miracle of the Mind." Sara also served as the Administrative Assistant for Computer Services at Cornell University's Graduate School of Business and Public Administration, as the Training Director for Data Processing for the State of New Mexico, taught sixth grade in Concord, California, and was the operations manager for Unisun, a solar energy company in Santa Fe, New Mexico.

On March 9, 1981, Christ appeared in her bedroom, put his hands on her head, and called her to a path that eventually led her to become the messenger for the Operation Terra Messages and mission. After being totally disabled by a collapse of her immune system in 1984, Sara began the long walk back to functionality and turned to writing as one of the few things she could do while living life as a "bubble person," allergic to nearly everything. Her articles were published in several New Age magazines, and when she was well enough to work again, she began providing freelance book production services for publishers and authors. She now lives in a remote area of the United States and the Hosts have now said that she will ascend onto the ships at the end of July 2005.

ABOUT THE PUBLISHER

CELESTIAL WAY publishes the Operation Terra material, both in print form and on the Web at www.operationterra.com. Due to the anticipated lifting of the first and second waves, there will be no one left to contact regarding these books or the information in them. The books are available throughout the world through print-on-demand technology, without the need for a publisher's representative being present on the planet to ship them. They are carried through major distribution channels worldwide and can also be viewed online through the Operation Terra Web site through July 2007 or as long as there is an Internet, whichever comes first.

There will be no one available to answer phones, mail, or questions after July 31, 2005. We wish you well on your journey, wherever it may lead and whatever form it may take.

Peace be with you,
Sara Lyara Estes

Printed in the United States
60542LVS00003B/158